Sarah McDonald
"BISHOP OF THE FIRST WARD"

Sarah McDonald, Jack, and Emma Marr

Sarah McDonald

"BISHOP OF THE FIRST WARD"

Peggy Petersen Barton & Drew Barton Quinn

ASPEN BOOKS

Sarah McDonald: "Bishop of the First Ward"

Copyright 1993 by Peggy Petersen Barton & Drew Barton Quinn
All rights reserved
7 February *Church News* article by Gordon B. Hinckley reprinted with
permission

Library of Congress Cataloging-in-Publication Data

    Barton, Peggy.
        Sarah M. McDonald: bishop of the First Ward /
        by Peggy Petersen Barton and Drew Barton Quinn.
            p. cm.
        ISBN 1-56236-211-9 : $10.95
        1. McDonald, Sarah, 1863-1957. 2. Relief Society
        (Church of Jesus Christ of Latter-day Saints)
        —Presidents—Biography. 3. Mormons—Utah—Biography.
        4. Mormons—Nova Scotia—Biography.
        I. Quinn, Drew Barton.
    II. Title.
    BX8695.M26B37 1993
    289.3'092—dc20   93-38204
    [B]   CIP

Printed in the United States of America

4 3 2

Designed by Yvonne M. Wright

Sarah McDonald

Gordon B. Hinckley
Church News 7 February 1948, page 2

Whistler's Mother. Yes, you might think so as she sits in her rocker in her front room. But no, there is a likelier personality from history with whom to compare her. Lincoln comes to mind. Sarah McDonald's tall, spare figure, her deep-set eyes that speak of understanding; her forthright, wise manner; her love of truth and justice—all these strengthen the parallel with the Great Emancipator.

Her circle has been limited. For the past thirty-four years she has lived in the First Ward of Salt Lake City. But everyone who has come in contact with her has felt the impact of her character.

For twelve of those years she served as president of the ward Relief Society. Neither snow, nor rain, nor sweltering heat kept her from her duty as she saw it. Food came to bare tables, children were clothed, kitchen fires were kept burning, and the sick were comforted and strengthened through her ministrations.

Since then the years have sapped her strength. But she is still a power in the Relief Society—and in everything else that goes on in the ward. She seldom misses a meeting and can make an intelligent contribution on almost any question that is asked.

For eighteen successive years she taught Sunday School. She also taught in the M.I.A. But her most extraordinary teaching position was as instructor of the High Priests class of the Sunday School. At that time the adult department of the Sunday School was divided on a quorum basis. The stake officers felt that a man ought to teach the class. But after listening to Sister Mac, as she is familiarly known, they knew the wisest choice had been made.

None of her students ever found himself a match for her on the Bible. Few have a better understanding of the gospel. None has a greater love for the Church.

That love is strong because Church membership was bought dearly.

Sarah McDonald was born in 1863 in a frontier village of Nova Scotia. Four Scottish brothers, one of them her father, had left the economic oppression of their native land to seek a better life in this New Scotland. Coupled with industry, they possessed the sterling virtues of minds and wills of their own. Sarah received from her proud father a remarkable heritage of individual thought and action which took her through one school after another until she became an outstanding teacher, which won her the love of a prominent sea captain, gave her the courage to fight for her convictions concerning the truths of Mormonism, and enabled her to walk boldly in the face of one of the most violent anti-Mormon campaigns ever leveled against an individual member of the Church.

After teaching school for six years in Nova Scotia, Sarah married Captain John McDonald, skipper of the *Emma Marr*. With him she traveled from one part of the world to another. Among her harrowing experiences was a shipwreck when the *Emma Marr* sank. With others who were aboard she sat in an open lifeboat tossed by heavy seas until a passing vessel picked them up. In the days before wireless telegraphy, an SOS signal could be sent only as far as a man could shout or a waving flag could be seen.

While Sarah and John McDonald were residing in Liverpool, another man of the sea boarded in their home for a time.

Somehow, somewhere he had heard of the Mormons, and eventually he was baptized. One day he brought his landlady two or three of the "Rays of Living Light" series of tracts. "Here," he told her, "read these when you have a little time. They won't hurt you."

Little did he realize that those tracts would steer her into new and troubled seas where she would feel for years the sharp barbs of persecution and bigotry.

Sarah McDonald was an educated woman who knew the Bible. And she knew the truth when she read it. Her husband resented this new religion which came into her life. Nonetheless, she accepted baptism at the hands of Elder John C. Duncan.

Immediately the storm broke loose over her head. Her Presbyterian friends turned against her. The newspapers carried venomous stories about this mother who had been snared in the Mormon net. But Sarah McDonald had made her decision, and nothing on earth could change it.

Persecution followed her when she returned home to Nova Scotia. Old friends greeted her, and then came back to hiss when they learned of her conversion. It was not easy to be the only member of the Church of Jesus Christ of Latter-day Saints within a radius of nine hundred miles, particularly when she was a constant target of attack. One of less solid fiber would have wilted in the battle.

When she moved to Salt Lake City, she settled in the First Ward, where she has been since. John C. Duncan, who had baptized her, lived there. He shortly became bishop of the ward, and for more than a quarter of a century, he remained bishop. Small wonder that he selected as president of the Relief Society this strong woman whom he knew had been tested in the fire of oppression, persecution, and loneliness. Where could one better be found to clothe the naked, to feed the hungry, to comfort the bereaved than she who had known want, and sorrow, and a heavy yoke because of the gospel of Jesus Christ?

For Sarah McDonald

Who would sing a song
About the women—
The weaker vessels?
Did you learn of
Sarah McDonald?
Her saga is written
Upon the hearts of her
Children
And upon their lives, too.
And upon the souls of
Weaker folk—those
Who need faith,
Strong faith—
And endurance.

She heard
And doubted not.
She forsook all she had
But faltered
Not.
Once her head was
Turned toward
Zion
She turned not
Back.

Who will say from what
Source
She gained her fortitude,
Her courage, her
Loyalty,
Devotion?
From the divine
God.

She savored the
Gospel.
It was good.

In her soul was poured
Active testimony,
Burning,
Impelling.
So, being what she was, she
Could not give less than
All she was,
All she had.

Now her testimony
Stands sealed.
Not with blood
But with her
Unfaltering
Loyalty,
Devotion,
Love.

To us—however weak—
Our memory of her
Bids us, too,
To never
Falter
Ever.

By S. Dilworth Young
From *Here Stand I—Looking*
Published by Deseret Book, 1963

Chronology

December, 1853	John Alexander McDonald born
Winter, 1854	John McDiarmid marries Flora McLean
March 26, 1863	Sarah McDiarmid born
Fall, 1875	Sarah enters school at Fourchu, Nova Scotia
Fall, 1877	Sarah enters the Sydney Academy
June, 1879	Sarah graduates from Sydney Academy
Fall, 1879	Sarah teaches at Black Brook, Nova Scotia
Fall, 1880–1889	Sarah teaches at Caledonia, Nova Scotia
Spring, 1884	Sarah meets John Alexander McDonald
October 12, 1889	John Alexander McDonald marries Sarah McDiarmid
July 13, 1890	John Alexander McDonald Jr. (Jack) born
November 27, 1892	The ship *Emma Marr* sinks
September 13, 1893	Emma Marr McDonald born
April 23, 1897	John McDiarmid dies
May, 1897	Sarah, Jack, and Emma Marr arrive in Liverpool
1903–1907	Heber J. Grant presides over England Mission, headquarters in Liverpool
May 25, 1904	Sarah baptized by John C. Duncan and confirmed by John H. Brinton
1908	Sarah, Jack, and Emma Marr return to Sydney, Nova Scotia
June 5, 1912	Emma Marr baptized and confirmed
August 2, 1912	Jack baptized and confirmed
Fall, 1913	Sarah, Jack, and Emma Marr arrive in Salt Lake City
August 30, 1923	Mark Edward Petersen and Emma Marr McDonald marry
July 8, 1927	John Alexander McDonald dies
October 31, 1928	Jack marries Adonna Hunt Ivory
1928–1940	Sarah serves as Relief Society President of First Ward, Liberty Stake
November 29, 1957	Sarah dies

Acknowledgements

Almost everyone seems to know a story about Sarah McDonald. Few women in her generation wielded such influence in the Church. None demonstrated more respect for the priesthood and its authority. Sarah's firm testimony of the truth of the gospel caused her to turn her back on the wealth of the world. Like the rich young ruler of the New Testament, she had accumulated much, yet she arrived in Salt Lake with only the clothes on her back and a cherished photograph of her husband.

Her strength fascinated her family. We felt that her Canadian childhood, the shipwreck, the tempestuous marriage, the persecution, the life-encompassing Church service should all be recorded. Our search led us to England, to the Maritime Museum at Greenwich, and to the records of Lloyds of London, insurer of the *Emma Marr* and subsequent ships captained by John Alexander McDonald. Discovery of Sarah's personal diary, which revealed so many of her thoughts and feelings, strengthened our determination to write this volume.

When Sarah settled in Zion she stopped writing regularly in her journal. Much of the material for the final chapters of this book came from personal interviews and the Relief Society minutes preserved at the LDS Church Historical Library.

Our thanks to Martin and Virginia Mitchell for their generous support, Harold and Naomi Goodman for direction and encouragement in London, Jake Garn who shared his memories of Sister McDonald and revived some of our own, Darla Isackson and Paul Rawlins for insightful editing, Elder Hugh Pinnock for his enthusiasm for the project, and especially President Gordon B. Hinckley who allowed us to use his *Church News* article written so many years ago.

Peggy Petersen Barton
Drew Barton Quinn

Chapter One

"The Lord is my shepherd. I shall not want."

Kneeling with her family in the firelight, seven-year-old Sarah listened as her father's voice swelled with emotion.

"He restoreth my soul."

Big John McDiarmid always read this beloved scripture with wet cheeks and a full heart. And Sarah smiled as the gentle farmer rolled his *r*'s, caressing with the sweet sounds of his Scottish burr the words of King David. "And I will dwell in the house of the Lorrrd foreverrrr."

Sarah, born March 26, 1863, was the elder of the two McDiarmid girls. She felt closest of all the children to her parents, although boisterous Archie and Matt preceded her in the family lineup. Her love of reading bound her to her studious father, in spite of his formal education having ended when he left the shores of his native Scotland bound for Canada. They had lived outside Sydney, in Nova Scotia, ever since Sarah could remember.

Settling back on her heels, Sarah watched the flickering shadows play on her father's face as he began the story that always followed his recitation of the 23rd Psalm—the story of the McDiarmids' beginnings.

"For generations our family had struggled for survival on North Uist, one of the outer Hebrides Islands. Landlord greed, heavy taxes, and repeated crop failures combined against us tenant farmers making it impossible to live decently, and the constabulary seemed always to be on the side of the rent collectors. Only the indomitable McDiarmid spirit and faith in God sustained us."

Memories of the pain and hardship, the misery, poverty, hunger, and cold momentarily overcame Big John, and his eyes glistened as he continued the tale in his native Gaelic.

"The Hebrides, forty miles off the west coast of Scotland, had many more people than they could support even though fewer than 100 of the 500 barren islands were settled. The outer Hebrides where the McDiarmids lived—Lewis, Harris, Barra, and our own Uist—lay as far north as Moscow, Russia, and seemed just as cold. Winter nights lasted twenty-two black hours. Peat burning on the cottage hearth offered the only relief from the gale's icy blasts, which penetrated cracks in walls and windows in spite of all efforts to keep them out.

"In the summer the family fished and farmed, and always we dug peat in the bogs. Year round the scent of peat fires hung on the air. Around us were glorious skies and surging seas and heather blooming on the moors in August. But the beauties of the landscape could not compensate for our family's constant hunger. Every cottage had a loom where the women wove the wool they had dyed and spun to fashion the rugged tweed fabric which protected us from cold and damp. Without animals of our own, we pulled wool from gorse bushes where sheep had passed, and these scraps of fluff became the clothes on our backs. Any extra bit of material went to market to be traded for food."

John McDiarmid paused and glanced with pride at his five well-fed, warmly dressed, healthy children, his smiling wife, and the snug log walls made with his own hands. Then he continued.

"When I was ten years of age, a neighbor asked me to accompany him on his little boat to the Isle of Lewis where he was to buy some sails. While he conducted his business, I left the harbor and climbed to the eerie Callanish Standing Stones. To me they seemed like a gathering of giant, gray old men stretching to the cloudy sky. My schoolmaster had called them the ultimate glory of the Hebrides. More than a little amazed and awed at their size and number, I thought them to be the ultimate glory of the world! Blackfaced sheep with curling horns freely roamed our islands. A large ghostly-eyed ewe resting near me bleated loudly for her wandering lamb. I had forgotten myself, so entranced with the Standing Stones was I, and at the sound of her call I bolted from the spot and never stopped running until I reached the harbor."

Little Sarah smiled as she imagined her dignified father, shirttails flying, racing away from a benign female sheep.

"We McDiarmids thought our lives hard enough with unforgiving soil and abusive landlords. Then came the masses from Ireland fleeing from their own starvation. Five Irish families crowded into one cottage in our village, and their willingness to accept the lowest of wages eliminated the last extra jobs which could have kept our hunger from turning to starvation. This torrent of immigrants from Ireland offering an unlimited supply of cheap labor dimmed our hopes for the future.

"From the black pit of despair we watched our potato crop fail. After a poor grain harvest and a drop in the price of cattle, the landlord gave our family a fortnight to vacate our century-old home. He had decided to clear all tenants from the land and replace them with more profitable sheep.

"With other families from the islands, we made our way to Glasgow, remaining there until the men could earn the family's boat passage. We had seen the roofs torn from our cottages and our neighbors huddled among their poor possessions at the roadside. These were our memories as we sailed from Glasgow to a new country where we prayed for adequate food and freedom from oppression. I was twelve years old when we set sail.

"Aboard the little ship I became acquainted with your mother and her family. Flora McLean was a bonny lass, only six years old. On our voyage, we wondered not a few times why we had left Scotland. We were crowded into the hold of a poorly built boat. We slept in narrow berths with little ventilation and were given insufficient food and water. The biweekly fumigation of the bedding with vinegar only added pungency to the human odors. Starvation, seasickness, and scurvy haunted the group, and I witnessed five burials at sea. True Scottish Presbyterians, we studied our Bibles, and not a day passed without a reading of the 23rd Psalm to comfort us. After the eight longest weeks of my life we landed at Sydney, a small, bleak country town on the rocky coast of Nova Scotia. Sandy beaches, twisted trees, and forty- to one hundred-foot bedrock cliffs appeared forbidding to a farmer yearning for flat land to till.

"Nothing there could tempt the McDiarmids to remain in Sydney, and after trading our few belongings for provisions we traveled twenty miles straight into the forest to the Framboise area. Not even a clearing greeted us. With my family I took up a large tract of land, nature in its roughest form. Together the nine of us built a log house consisting of one room, one window, a dirt floor, moss-chinked walls, a rude fireplace with an opening in the ceiling above to let out the smoke, and a bark roof thatched with spruce boughs. More spruce boughs served as our beds. We planted potatoes and corn, snared rabbits and shot partridges and ducks for meat, but the first year we went to bed aching with hunger most of the time. Following four winter months when the temperature never climbed above zero, we replanted our potatoes. One of us used the hand plow while the others followed, flipping over the heavy sod between the roots of trees felled the previous autumn for our cabin. The second year we planted oats. After the third winter the stumps had rotted enough to begin the unending task of clearing the fields of wood and stones. With prayer and tireless labor our seeds grew. But it was three hard years before we had enough food, or even ample wood to keep our fires burning brightly.

"Then my brothers married. We built log houses fine enough to be proud of for each of their brides and later built a one-room schoolhouse as the children began to come along. The four of us took turns teaching what we knew of the three Rs and daily studied the Bible and *Pilgrim's Progress* with our young charges.

"Twice weekly we attended the nearest Presbyterian church, where I watched Flora McLean, my little friend from the ocean voyage, grow from an apple-cheeked imp to a tall, slender, beautiful young woman. Her blue eyes always sparkled with mischief, even when I begged her to be my bride, and she wondered aloud why I had taken so long in asking. Hand in hand we walked twelve miles through waist-deep snow in the winter of 1854 to a place called Grand River where we were married. A blizzard overtook us on the way home, and the twelve miles seemed like twelve thousand. Our little one-room log house was a most welcome sight, particularly when we saw smoke curling from its chimney. My brothers and their wives had kept a fire banked for two days awaiting our return. An abundance of dried meat, vegetables, and firewood appeared miraculously from well-wishers. Newly made homespun sheets and two new patchwork quilts covered our bed. And you know the rest," he concluded.

Catherine and Donald had crept nearer the fire and, huddled together, slept contentedly. Sarah wondered how they could fall asleep before the end of the story, but of course Catherine had just turned four and baby Donald was only one. Big John McDiarmid raised his voice in prayer.

"We thank thee, O Lord, for all our bounty: for food, for clothes, for warmth, for health, and for thy beloved Book of King James, the Holy Bible. Amen. Goodnight, children."

Archie, Matt, and Sarah meekly tiptoed after their father, who held a sleeping child in each of his huge arms. They knew that their mother, Flora, would soon come to hear their prayers and bring heated stones for their feet. Through a tiny window above her candlelit bed Sarah watched the stars, convinced that she was the luckiest girl in the whole wide world.

Chapter Two

Sarah woke to the aroma of pork crackling on the fire. If no snow had fallen during the night she and her two brothers could walk atop the frozen drifts to the school two miles distant. Always grateful for a clear sky, she pulled up the long underwear and heavy stockings her mother had knit for her. Next she slipped the soft woolen petticoat over her head, followed by a rough, brown homespun dress. She snatched her shoes and, holding her breath against the cold, raced to the fire in the great room to button them near the fire's radiant warmth. She braided her waist-length, black hair into one fat pigtail; then, neatly dressed, Sarah was ready to kneel beside her chair at the table as her father thanked God for his goodness. After breakfast, in a flurry of boots, scarves, and mittens, the older McDiarmids left for school, Archie and Matt leading Sarah on a merry chase. Two miles passed quickly with animal tracks to investigate, snow-laden branches to shake, streams to jump, and birds to watch.

Sarah felt proud as they approached the new schoolhouse. Colorful maps and slate blackboards adorned the walls. A potbelly stove glowed in the center of the room where teacher and students alike huddled gratefully on cold days. The benches seated three or four students, and the working surfaces for their desks were nailed to the back of the benches in front of them. This close proximity had led more than once to Archie's dunking

Sarah's long braid in his inkwell. One day he put his frozen bottle of ink on the school stove. The bottle shattered and sent a cascade of black liquid and broken glass onto the rough floor.

Books were scarce, but varied, and each child had his own text by W. R. Mulholland. The Bible and *Pilgrim's Progress* were read daily at home, and Sarah especially enjoyed the quaint names given to the *Pilgrim's Progress* characters, like By-ends, Ignorance, and Faithful.

"I attended school faithfully, missing only the snowiest days. After learning to read I seldom returned home without a new volume tucked under my coat," she would tell her grandchildren. Schoolmaster Roddie Ferguson took turns boarding at each of his pupil's homes. School fascinated Sarah, and early on he had recognized her scholastic ability and looked forward eagerly to his visits with her. Big John McDiarmid felt determined to provide an education for each of his children. If the family scholar happened to be a female, so be it. Sarah would be given every opportunity for the best training available.

In the summertime, the children helped with farm and household duties. Sarah learned to sew, knit, and mind the younger children. Chores for the boys included going for the sheep or cows, picking rocks out of the fields, carrying water, and milking. But there was also time for games—magical hours of play. Woods with swimming holes beckoned the children, and they frequently enjoyed berry picking. When the snow fell, coasting, skating, and building snow houses for snowball wars were favorite pastimes. Telling ghost stories and playing games such as hide-and-seek and blindman's bluff also helped fill the free hours.

A horse and wagon or sleigh carried the McDiarmids to worship at the nearest Presbyterian church, six miles distant, in Loch Lomund. They attended at least one service each Sunday, but as the five children grew and began to fill the wagon to overflowing, Archie, Matt, and Sarah took turns walking. Always they found fascinating animals and birds along the dirt track. To Sarah it seemed the bushes were mainly inhabited by snakes. Two kinds were common: small greens that liked the water and large ones, gray-mottled and vicious. The brothers tried to kill at least one snake each time they traveled to and from church. A Sunday without a dead snake was not considered a success. The boys used rocks to attack their prey. The only member of the family who possessed a gun was Big John, and he left his firearm at home on Sunday. Carrying a gun was considered a serious breach of the Sabbath, and shooting was unpardonable, even in a life-and-death situation.

The years passed happily for the McDiarmids, with Flora and Big John teaching their children to pray, to study, to work, and to treat their family and friends with honesty and kindness.

When Sarah turned twelve, the schoolmaster appeared on the McDiarmid doorstep. Sarah was already as tall as her elder brothers, and her mind had kept pace with her body. Now Mr. Ferguson felt he could no longer cope with the responsibility of her education. Each of the other McDiarmid children thirsted for knowledge and led their peers in the schoolroom, but Sarah led the *schoolmaster*, asking questions he could not answer. "If at twelve she has devoured all the information available to her, what of future years?" asked Mr. Ferguson.

The teacher's visit surprised and disturbed Big John, whose own formal education had ended at age twelve, although he had continued to borrow books whenever he was able. Even the most tattered volume filled him with awe and excitement. Because of his constant efforts to read and learn, he was considered the resident scholar of Framboise. But what of his daughter? Should she pursue further education? If she left home to expand her mind, would she, could she, ever comfortably return? Was it possible to create a Sarah too educated to be happy?

Whenever Big John needed to think, he went off into the woods alone and stayed on his knees until his Heavenly Father gave him an answer. Late March in Nova Scotia with snow still on the ground seemed an unlikely time for such meditation, but with an extra saddle blanket Sarah's father rode away from the farm on his favorite black horse. Two hours later when he returned, he knew what he must do.

Following evening prayers, Big John asked Sarah to remain with him while her mother helped the other children prepare for bed. Sarah often enjoyed long talks with her father and looked forward to time alone together. But now his solemn expression worried her, and Sarah wondered if she had done something to make him unhappy.

"You are twelve years old," her father began, "a young lady." Sarah smiled and straightened her back, sitting the way she imagined a young lady might sit. In the firelight she could be a young Flora, Big John thought, surprised at the lump in his throat.

"Sarah, how would you like to go to school?"

Puzzled, she replied, "I already go to school, Father."

"Would you like to attend a more advanced school, a school in Fourchu?" her father continued. "Fourchu is a village where the people make their living by fishing. There is a large lobster factory with many workers. The fresh lobster only a few minutes out of the sea has a special taste that cannot be described. Because of all the factory people, there is a wonderful school at Fourchu." He faltered. How could he send Sarah into the arms of strangers—Sarah who had never been away from her family? But Sarah's reaction astounded him.

"A real school, Father? A school where I could learn everything?" In her excitement her pretense of being a young lady vanished, and she jumped onto her father's lap.

"So it is decided," Big John murmured softly. "In the autumn I will take you to Fourchu."

That fall Sarah found herself in an unfamiliar classroom, conscious of the curious stares of the girls on either side of her. She realized that although she wore the nicest dress she owned, her appearance was quite different from those around her. A young man behind her snickered and pointed at her clumsy boots. But when Mr. McDonald, the instructor, entered the room and the pupils stood at attention, Sarah's discomfort vanished. She answered every question correctly even though she seemed to be several years younger than any other student. In the following months Sarah felt as if Mr. McDonald lectured only for her. Still, she did not feel accepted by her classmates and ate all her meals alone. The others sat in their own groups and no one invited the little girl from the backwoods to join them. But after blessing her food (as she had promised her father she would do), she always read as she ate. In a way she felt relieved that she needn't sacrifice mealtimes to chitchat with her classmates.

At home Sarah had shared her bed with Catherine. On the coldest of nights, back-to-back with her sister with heated stones at their feet, a rush of gratitude and well-being had warmed "the cockles of her heart" as her father always said. At school she slept alone in a narrow cot—one of a long row of cots occupied by strangers, girls whose manner and dress were foreign to her. Sarah's love-filled world had become unfriendly, and lonely tears often dampened her pillow at night.

Gradually, the days seemed easier to bear. From the time she arrived at the classroom until Mr. McDonald dismissed them, the wonder of learning exhilarated Sarah. Her nervous glances at the loudly ticking schoolroom clock behind the teacher's desk stemmed from the hope that she still had time for just one more project, one more page.

After two years Big John McDiarmid again was confronted with an anxious instructor. Mr. McDonald announced that Sarah had learned all there was to learn at the Fourchu school. Effortlessly, she had completed a four-year course in two years, receiving the highest marks in her class as well as first prize in public speaking. At fourteen years of age she had prepared herself to enter the Sydney Academy.

Sarah's first day at the Academy was filled with amazement at all the fine young men and women—city folk. She felt frightened until the principal, Burgess McKettrick, expressed his pleasure at having her attend his institution, commenting on her excellent record at Fourchu. The friendly students offered welcoming handshakes and genuine concern to this shy, green girl from the backwoods of Nova Scotia where the very name *academy* was unknown. In a letter home Sarah described the Sydney school as a "superb learning opportunity with a large staff of well grounded teachers." She enjoyed three blissful years among seasoned students and accomplished educators. She was ecstatically happy.

In 1879 in a blossom-filled June, Sarah graduated number one in her class amid the cheers of her family and fellow students. The ceremony was marred only by the absence of her mother, still home recuperating from the recent and difficult birth of baby Alexia four months before.

Following graduation, the Academy placed Sarah in an excellent beginning teaching position in a remote inland village called Black Brook. As a teacher of fifteen to twenty pupils in a one-room schoolhouse, Sarah wondered how she would learn the students' names until she realized that they were all either Miss or Mr. Morrison except for one McLean.

Sarah had no home of her own, but boarded with the pupils' families, where she discovered that poverty and happiness can dwell together. The Morrisons were kind and free with the few possessions they had, gladly sharing with this attractive young instructor.

One year later Sarah received an offer to teach in a better, larger school at Caledonia, only three miles from her parents' farm. Sarah happily returned to her family, much to the delight of young baby Lexie. Because Big John and her brothers were usually busy with the horses, Sarah walked to school daily, thinking the hike a small price to pay for the privilege of living in her own home.

One day a fellow schoolmarm proposed a trip to Halifax to see her parents, the shops, and the big city sights. Sarah eagerly accepted, never guessing that her world would never be the same.

Her first view of many-storied buildings and bustling wharves fascinated the young girl. She had taught her pupils about Halifax and knew all the facts: Halifax was the capital of Nova Scotia, its largest city, and a valuable Canadian port because the harbor rarely froze over or was blocked by ice. Halifax had begun as a fortress in 1749, and as Sarah climbed the hill to the fort overlooking the harbor, she smiled as she imagined the colorful lesson she could give on her return. The boys would be speechless at her description of the cannons. And the girls would never believe the merchandise in the shops. The variety of goods in the stores made Sarah wish for funds to buy presents for every member of her family.

Sarah was grateful that her personal shopping had been so successful and that she was wearing smart new clothes when her hostess called from the parlor, "Sarah, come sit with my guest while I bring the tea."

Sarah dutifully entered the room, expecting an elderly

clergyman or the lady next door. Instead a tall, lean, dark-haired naval officer stood near the fire. His mind proved to be as bright as the brass buttons on his uniform, and his friends called him "Big John," just like her father. Sarah held her breath until she established that he was in fact a Big John McDonald, not a Big John McDiarmid.

"Wouldn't you enjoy a walk to the park? It's a shame to hide such beauty in the house," Big John said, with a tinge of gentle humor in his deep voice.

For the first time in her life she couldn't utter a word. Mutely, Sarah, winner of public speaking awards in two schools, simply nodded yes. Big John McDonald talked easily of his travels to Liverpool, England. As she listened, Sarah recalled her geography lessons, amazed that they could come alive in John's words. He spoke of the sights and sounds of London, the parks, the people, and the River Thames. Was it this sailor's vivid descriptions which fascinated her or his equally vivid blue eyes locking with hers as he said goodnight?

Tossing in her unfamiliar bed, Sarah recalled each word of their conversation. She and Big John shared so many things— both born in Framboise, both Scottish Presbyterians, both voracious readers. She felt that Providence had directed her to Halifax for this meeting.

The next morning, the doorbell brought Sarah flying down the stairs, certain that she knew who would be standing on the stoop. She checked her speed abruptly and peered into the hall tree's dark mirror. Bright eyes and flushed cheeks greeted her blue-eyed gaze. Sedately, Sarah opened the door and invited her new friend into the parlor.

"Could you walk to the park with me again, Sarah? My orders have come; I am leaving tonight and we have so much to say. Sarah, do you believe in destiny?"

Chapter Three

For weeks Sarah had longed for a ride to Sydney, so when Archie announced plans to drive into town on a school holiday she offered her company. Sarah steeled herself against Archie's scornful comments about her "Halifax outfit," but on that day her brother's only reaction seemed to be admiring silence. Traveling together in a horse-drawn wagon, Archie and Sarah soon began to trade memories of other rides and other times. Archie had always hidden snakes and frogs in the back of the wagon, evoking terrified shrieks and laughter.

Sarah wondered if she should tell her brother of the paralysis which seemed to afflict her whenever she thought of John McDonald. Her teaching had always been of prime importance. Now when sailing ships or far-off places arose in a lesson, her heart pounded, she felt breathless, and she usually lost her train of thought. Would Archie understand that Sarah sometimes felt as if she should be perched in the corner on a stool wearing her own dunce cap? Perhaps not, so the brother and sister spoke of fun, farm, and family until they reached the outskirts of town where Archie deposited his favorite sibling near her alma mater.

Strolling down the main street of Sydney, Sarah was conscious of the approving glances of passersby. Critically she appraised her appearance in the window of Wadsworth's Mercantile, noting the close fit of her long, black wool coat; the

smartly rolled silk umbrella; the broad-brimmed, veiled hat
perching on her upswept black hair. Even her gleaming patent
shoes had come straight from Halifax, and she felt sure that no
one could guess that they had been made for a man's foot.
Sarah hated to buy shoes, knowing that the clerk inevitably
would exclaim at the length of her size-eleven feet. But nothing
could spoil her mood as she approached the Sydney Academy,
wondering how it could possibly be five years since her graduation.

Relieved to see Mr. McKettrick sitting alone reading in his
office, Sarah rapped on the open door and was met by his
wide smile. "Could this grand lady be related to the frightened
Miss McDiarmid who entered the Academy in 1877?" the
principal teased. "And would you have an idea where she has
gone?" he continued.

All hesitation vanished as Sarah told her dear friend about
her adventures since graduation, the Morrisons at Black Brook;
the promotion to a better, larger school at Caledonia; the joy of
living at home again. Then the trip to Halifax, the first in her life,
and the wonders of the large city tumbled out. She even
confided her feelings concerning Captain John Alexander
McDonald. Her confusion finally found expression, as Sarah
read affection and concern in the wise eyes of Mr. McKettrick.

"What has happened to my teaching, and why can't I keep
my mind on my lessons?" Sarah moaned. "Am I like the awful girls
I watch at church on Sundays vying for my brothers' attentions?"

Mr. McKettrick reached for a newly arrived volume of
Keats' poems and turning to his bookmark at "Isabella" read
aloud, "'He might not in house, field, or garden stir, but her full
shape would all his seeing fill.'" It had not occurred to Sarah
that Big John might be experiencing the same confusion she
felt. Mr. McKettrick continued, "'And his continual voice was
pleasanter to her, than noise of trees or hidden rill; Her

lute-string gave an echo of his name, She spoilt her half-done broidery with the same.' So you see, Sarah, they are having the same trouble as you all the way across the Atlantic Ocean in England. And let me read again:

> A *whole long month of May in this sad plight*
> *Made their cheeks paler by the break of June:*
> *"To-morrow will I bow to my delight,*
> *Tomorrow will I ask my lady's boon."*
> *"O may I never see another night,*
> *Lorenzo, if thy lips breathe not love's tune."*
> *So spake they to their pillows; but, alas,*
> *Honeyless days and days did he let pass."*

Sarah had heard brief mention of Keats in a poetry class, but had never before seen his published work. Mr. McKettrick tended to hide from public view his passion for the new poetry. He opened his desk drawer and withdrew another volume, also modern, containing the writings of Lord Byron. "'She walks in beauty like the night of cloudless climes and starry skies; And all that's best of dark and bright Meet in her aspect and her eyes,'" he read aloud.

"Captain McDonald may be thinking such thoughts, standing on the deck at night watching the starry skies. Don't worry about your feelings or confusion. When the time comes for him to ask his question you will know your answer. My brightest pupil won't hesitate to give the correct response." The old man closed the book and rose from his desk. With a grateful smile, Sarah offered him her cheek and, promising to keep in touch, left the room.

"Where was Archie?" Sarah wondered as she paced back and forth in front of Wadsworth's—Archie who was always so punctual. Had she misunderstood that he would meet her with the wagon at 2 p.m.? The time on Sarah's pocket watch, hanging on its black ribbon, was already 3 p.m. Fear of an accident troubled Sarah's mind. By 3:30 Sarah felt certain Archie must be dead. Never in his life had he been even a minute late for an appointment, he was such a man of his word. Just as Sarah decided to organize a search for him, her brother swung round the corner, the wagon on two wheels, and pulled up directly in front of her. Judging from the lather on the horses and the high color on Archie's cheeks, they had covered a considerable distance in a short time.

Wondering where he had been and what he had been doing, Sarah climbed to the high seat beside him. Archie raised his hat, smiled sedately, and slowly turned the rig toward the road home. After several miles of restrained silence Sarah could contain her curiosity no longer. "Where *have* you been and what *have* you been doing?" she demanded.

Archie announced sheepishly, "I've met a girl." As Sarah examined her brother's face a deep crimson blush began at his collar and spread with astonishing rapidity to his hairline. Archie and a girl—Sarah could scarcely believe it. Hardworking, serious Archie, object of frank admiration from the entire unmarried female population of their neighborhood. Archie whose scorn for girls was equalled only by his attitude toward cowards and highway robbers—Archie and a real live girl?

"Sarah, I know you don't understand what I am about to tell you, but someday you will when you are a little older and have met someone special, someone wonderful, someone different from anyone else you have ever known."

Smiling to herself, Sarah thought of someone special, someone wonderful, someone different from anyone she had ever known, and she began to laugh.

"Don't start your laughing," Archie accused. "It isn't funny."

"Oh yes, it is funny," his sister retorted. "I have bounced twenty miles on a rutted dirt road to speak to a person I hoped would understand this very problem, and for twenty miles I sat next to a person talking only about the farm."

Archie turned to her in amazement. Sarah, all decked out in her grown-up outfit, Sarah who had always been his little sister. He had to admit that he had noticed her absent gaze at mealtimes lately, a bemused kind of a glow he had never before seen.

"Archie," Sarah began sweetly, "tell me about your girl."

For miles her brother expounded on the wonders of romance, new feelings previously unknown and undreamed of, the surge of hope and happiness followed by an exquisite pang of fear or loneliness.

"Oh, Archie." Sarah's white hand crept over her brother's rough leather glove where he held the reins. "Archie, now let me tell you my story."

In a quiet voice Sarah described her trip to Halifax and the meeting with Captain McDonald, the shock of hearing of another man called Big John, of wondering if this could be a sign, of fearing that she might not be noticed. Breathlessly she explained the feeling in the pit of her stomach when his eyes bored into hers as he said good-bye. Even though she had not seen him for three long months, the emotions overwhelming her seemed ever more intense.

The two McDiarmids talked themselves home, covering the twenty miles with their longings. "I wonder if Mother waited dinner for us. I think she did," Archie surmised, "because all the lights are blazing." He drove to the barn to unhitch the horses, telling his sister that she looked much too fine to help.

Sarah hurried up the steps and into the parlor to find herself gazing into the same blue eyes she had been dreaming of, those of Captain John Alexander McDonald!

Chapter Four

Flora McLean McDiarmid had observed her daughter Sarah's behavior following her first trip to Halifax. Gentle probing determined the probable cause, a brief meeting with a young naval officer. Flora had sailed across the Atlantic ocean as a six-year-old, never complaining, accepting conditions that devastated many older children. Her ramrod-straight back declared to the world that behind the gentle smile lay determination and courage. Flora's husband was known as a backwoods intellectual, but no one guessed that his wife read by candlelight, late at night when the family slept, every book which Big John brought home.

As Sarah's prodigious mental ability revealed itself in her schoolwork, family members became accustomed to ascribing intelligence as a gift from the McDiarmid side of the family, declaring her to be "just like her father." Flora, secure in her understanding that she too possessed a brilliant mind, tended to keep her thoughts to herself. She alone knew that bright Sarah was even more like her mother.

When the handsome seaman had appeared on her doorstep, Flora, feeling that she had endured Sarah's mooning long enough, invited him into the parlor and offered him a friendly cup of tea. Grateful to examine firsthand a man who might possibly join her family, smiling Flora relieved his obvious nervousness while probing his background. She learned he was the son of a Presbyterian minister and a believer, which was of first importance. He had reached the top of his profession early, as the captain, or master, of the *Emma Marr*[1], a wood barque. Though small, it was a fine ship which the owner often used for his personal travel. Flora felt this to be a compliment to captain and vessel. John McDonald spoke of his background without boasting. He told of his devotion to his widowed mother and his regret that he could not see her more often. Two cups of tea later Sarah's mother was convinced that the young man sitting before her was a jewel—honest, bright, considerate, successful, Presbyterian—and possibly even good enough for her Sarah.

The family wagon pulled into the yard, and John's blush revealed the same overwhelming emotions that Sarah seemed to feel. The flush of pleasure on Sarah's face when she discovered their visitor removed any possible doubt. With amusement, Flora observed her ebullient daughter struck totally dumb. Captain McDonald, possessed of a silver tongue until Sarah's appearance, now had difficulty with a simple "Hello." Archie's arrival broke the spell, and the three young people followed Flora to the table where thick slices of homemade buttered bread, called "doorstops" by the McDiarmids, waited with a tureen of rich vegetable soup.

Halfway through the meal Archie caught Sarah's eye with a mischievous wink, and he asked Captain McDonald what brought him from his Sydney home twenty miles into the woods.

"Your sister Sarah," John said simply. "We met briefly in Halifax three months ago before my last voyage. I have thought of little else. I have a strong feeling that she is the girl I will marry."

No one spoke. No one knew quite what to say. Embarrassed and uncertain, Sarah and John started to speak at the same time, excused themselves, and fell silent. Again together they spoke. Flora interrupted them. "Before you children get married you should get acquainted. Please, John, stay with us for the weeks until you must return to your ship."

[1] The name *Emma Marr* was given to the ship by James Marr, the builder.

While Sarah taught school during the days that followed, John showed the four McDiarmid males that he was called Big John for good reason. Handling lines on a sailing vessel built muscular arms and climbing masts did wonders for the legs. Even though John was captain of his ship, his love of physical exertion kept him active, and it was not unusual for him to work side by side with his crew. Now on the McDiarmid farm laboring side by side with Sarah's father and three brothers, he kept pace with their exertions seemingly without effort.

Each afternoon he walked the three miles to Sarah's school and waited for her in the clearing. Each afternoon, it seemed to take the couple longer to return to the McDiarmid farm as they compared a lifetime of experiences, John fascinating Sarah with his travel and the favorite books he had read aboard ship, Sarah hardly daring to believe that she had actually found a friend as entranced with study as she. Evenings were filled with boisterous meals as each member of the McDiarmid clan, even five-year-old Lexie, entertained the captain by recounting family adventures. Two weeks later when Archie and John took the long wagon ride into Sydney—John to bid his mother good-bye, Archie to spend an afternoon with his sweetheart—Sarah had solemnly promised to wait for her sailor, a promise she would keep until the day she died.

The orders for Captain John McDonald aboard the *Emma Marr* at Halifax announced a promotion. His ship was now to sail between Canada and Brazil, in South America. Although pleased that he and his crew had received this prestigious new assignment, John felt disappointed that the change would prevent him from seeing Sarah more often than every six months. He was torn between land and sea. What if Sarah tired of waiting for him? Would she tolerate his lengthy absences? How could he tie her to him? With sweet nostalgia John recalled their walks together from her school to the McDiarmid farm. Three miles had been too short a distance to say all that needed saying. His letters could express his thoughts and feelings with the added advantage that they might be read and reread as often as Sarah desired.

Sitting at his desk in the captain's cabin, he gazed into the smiling eyes of the young school teacher in the photo in its silver frame. The frame had held another McDonald bride-to-be, his mother. It was her wish that Sarah's picture should now fill this place of honor and accompany John wherever he sailed. Taking up his pen, he began, "Dear Sarah." No, something was missing. "My dear Sarah" sounded like a bill collector, not someone addressing his darling girl. So it was that "Darling Sarah" became his special form of address whenever he spoke or wrote to his sweetheart.

✳

Darling Sarah,

I am writing to tell you that I purchased a small volume of John Keats' poetry which I shall deliver to you at your home in a fortnight. Although it has been three months since last we spoke, your letters awaited me in Brazil and as I read them I could hear your voice and see your face. I am delighted that your teaching goes well, that you find it so rewarding, and that your family enjoys good health and good spirits. So Archie is engaged to be married! How I envy him, but of course we must abide by your parents' wishes and postpone our nuptials until they are satisfied that we have become fully acquainted. However, if we are to spend as much time courting as did your brother and his sweetheart, with my limited leave we may find ourselves old and gray before reaching the altar. I have passed the evening on the bridge gazing at the stars. Before I met you, darling girl, all I observed in the heavens pertained to celestial navigation. I feel your nearness as now I know you search the same skies. My fervent prayer is that we may spend an eternity together.

Affectionately,
John

Chapter Five

"You're going to wear them out, Sarah," Lexie complained.

"Lexie, leave your sister alone," Flora admonished, not for the first time.

Carefully, twenty-six-year-old Sarah tied the letters into a neat bundle. She had chosen a navy satin ribbon from the vast array in Wadsworth's. It was the same blue as John's uniform and seemed just right. The days lasted a hundred hours now that she wasn't teaching, but the superintendent had been very firm—if her wedding date was October 12 she should not begin the term. A new teacher sat at Sarah's desk in the school at Caledonia. Sarah counted the seconds until John's return.

John . . . five years of waiting for him. Five years of letters flying back and forth across the Atlantic. Knowing that the *Emma Marr* was a gallant little ship helped to soothe her worries about his safety, and Sarah vowed that if ever she bore a daughter, her name would be Emma Marr. "Emma Marr McDonald, Sarah McDonald," Sarah experimented with the sounds. "John Alexander and Sarah McDiarmid McDonald were wed the twelfth of October 1889 in Sydney, Nova Scotia."

"Mother, Sarah's talking to herself again," Lexie declared with glee. "Mother, come and hear her," Lexie implored with the tenacity of a ten-year-old. Alexia, born sixteen years after Sarah, adored her and was often accused of being Sarah's shadow.

"Lexie, you tell Sarah to stop mooning right this minute. There's a handsome sailor approaching our doorstep," her mother called with a smile, "and he might change his mind about marrying her if he discovers that she spends all her time talking to herself."

Now Lexie raced to the door, pulled it open, and hurled herself at the approaching captain, very nearly knocking him to the ground.

Disengaging her future bridegroom from the loving tangle of her little sister's arms and legs, Sarah placed her hand in his, and silently they walked toward their favorite garden seat. Neither had experienced any emotion as strong as that now binding them together, and their firm belief in God and his plan assured them that their union was truly made in heaven. John felt frustrated as he tried to explain to his darling Sarah that the warmth of their love was a tangible physical presence, even on the bridge of the *Emma Marr*. He relaxed as she assured him that she understood, and had felt it too.

That they were together, never again to be parted, seemed incomprehensible. The owner of the *Emma Marr* allowed wives to sail with their captains, so Sarah McDiarmid, the girl from the backlands of Framboise, was to become Sarah McDonald, world traveler.

Sitting on the old maple bench huddled together against the cold, red leaves blowing, birds calling, twilight darkening the sky, John and Sarah exchanged promises never to be forgotten: John her only love, Sarah his only wife.

Nervously, Sarah anticipated meeting John's mother. His father, a Scottish Presbyterian minister, had, like the McDiarmids, regretfully left his homeland and arrived in Sydney filled with disappointment. Also like the McDiarmids, Donald and Catherine McDonald traveled to the Framboise area of

Nova Scotia, where their son John was born. Soon a church position became available in Pictou, a fishing village, where they moved to shepherd the parish. After ten satisfying years of service, the Reverend McDonald died and Catherine retired to Sydney with her son.

John and Sarah never seemed to be in Sydney at the same time, and since John felt strongly that introducing the two most important women in his life should be his own special privilege, Sarah and Catherine had never met. Now with the wedding just three days away the time had come, and as the McDiarmid wagon approached the McDonald cottage, Sarah's discomfort grew. What if she didn't like his mother? What if his mother disliked her? Sarah, whose self-confidence often bordered on pride, felt neither self-confident nor proud. In fact she was miserable.

Catherine McDonald nervously paced her spotless parlor, inspecting the Turkish rug for lint, admiring the soft sheen of the dark wooden floor, and moving a pillow to cover the worn spot on the sofa. Why couldn't Donald be here to greet this stranger who was to marry their John? At the sound of a wagon stopping outside, Catherine peeked through the white lace curtains. She saw a tall, elegant young lady in a long black coat. She had upswept hair topped by a ridiculous veiled hat. "Oh, Donald," she murmured, "why did you leave me at a time like this?"

But when the young couple entered the room, happiness radiating from their faces, Catherine felt content. She sensed that she would not live many years more. The hardships in North Uist had taken their toll on her health as it had her husband's. What greater gift could she receive than the assurance that her dear youngest child had a companion loved and as loving as her own. "It's all right Donald," she thought. "It's all right."

Aware of John's affection for his mother, Sarah hoped that her new mother-in-law would accept her with warmth. She was not disappointed. In a very few minutes Mrs. McDonald discovered that Sarah had a brother Donald, a sister Catherine, and a reverence for her parents' homeland of North Uist. As a small child, John's intellectual bent had appeared almost as soon as he could talk. How pleasing that Sarah prized this trait and shared his interests. And she came from a religious home. How very promising.

The visit ended with Archie's appearance at the door. He and Sarah would return to Framboise in the wagon, while John stayed with his mother in Sydney. As they began their long journey home, Archie raised an eyebrow at his unpredictable sister who jubilantly sang at the top of her lungs, "Pull for the Shore, Sailor, Pull for the Shore."

"Yes mum," Archie muttered under his breath. "Yes mum, Miss Sarah."

✳ ✳ ✳

The minister's ringing voice carried to the farthest pews in the little church, but only the first two rows were occupied. Reverend John Murray pronounced the couple man and wife. The mothers cried. The sisters kissed the bride. The brothers clapped the groom on the back and shook his hand. With a spotless white handkerchief, Big John McDiarmid carefully removed an imaginary speck from his moist eyes. Arm in arm, the newlyweds marched up the aisle and through the door without a backward glance.

That evening aboard the *Emma Marr*, Sarah watched brilliant stars above softly splashing waves, remembering all the nights as a child when she had studied the same skies from her little bed. Even then she felt a sense of mystery and awe as she gazed at the heavens hoping that they might reveal the future or the past. Sarah knew God lived somewhere above her. If she looked long enough and hard enough would she see his face? Was he the angry God of the Old Testament? Should she fear him? She thought not. The love she felt flowing from the heavens as she prayed convinced her that her Father in Heaven was kind and caring.

She could just make out John silhouetted on the bridge against the darkness. Oh, but she loved him! She hugged herself to contain the surge of emotion that swept over her whenever he was near. And now that she was the very important wife of a very important sea captain, he was nearby always.

"Our Father which art in Heaven," Sarah began. "I always seem to pray when I am happiest or saddest," she mused. "Where are you, Father in Heaven? Where is your star?"

Chapter Six

"Push, Sarah, push." Sarah's mother wiped her brow and regarded her worriedly.

"Push or the child will never come."

"I don't know how, Mother. A sailor's wife is born to pull, pull for the shore."

Poor, exhausted little girl, her mother thought. She's out of her head with the pain. Sarah grimaced as she hummed the tune that represented for her the new life she led. No more could she be considered a farm girl or a backlands girl or even a teacher. Her home was a ship and the ship's master her master. Pain washed over her in waves. Steady as you go. Why won't the pains stop? How can one endure such terrible torture? But I won't scream. I won't. Where is John? I have to find John. Shuddering, she tore at the clammy sheet that covered her. She wished it were warm and dry, instead of drenched with perspiration. Now I understand why they call this labor. Pull for the shore.

After two days of misery, with one last wracking spasm, Sarah McDiarmid McDonald delivered a black-haired baby boy, another John Alexander. When Flora placed the swaddled wee one in her arms, Sarah carefully examined her wondrous infant. He seemed to have all the necessary parts. Relieved, she lay back on the pillow holding him close.

So much had happened in the last year. She and John honeymooned on board the *Emma Marr*, bound for Cork, Ireland. Depending on wind for speed, the ship often lay becalmed. Just as it seemed the breezes had deserted them forever, a storm arose—the worst in John's memory. Violent weather and the rough ocean forced the sailors to throw the lumber on deck overboard. But even with the deck cleared, the heavy seas shifted the load remaining in the hold, causing the ship to list and take on water. After the storm, John held Sarah close, telling her that her first passage had been his roughest. He was proud of her courage and glad she was his wife. How astonishing after the gale to sail peacefully up the waters of the River Lee to the city of Cork.

With storm damage to the *Emma Marr* needing immediate attention, Sarah and John had found themselves in Ireland for six heavenly weeks—a real honeymoon. It had been the happiest of times, enhanced by the smiling hospitality of the Irish people. To Sarah's delight, she and John visited the old Blarney Castle where, although she did not actually kiss the stone, she saw it done, "not wanting to lean over the wall of the castle to accomplish the task," she wrote home. The guide explained that the stone had a magic influence and those who kissed it would ever be blessed with wit, a gift for oratory, and many other desirable characteristics. John gave the guide a coin and explained that his bride already possessed all of those traits.

When the repair of the *Emma Marr* was complete, they set sail for Canada, and a stowaway was discovered on board—a fifteen-year-old Irish boy named Jimmie Whistler. Before many days had passed, a storm as violent as the last attacked the ship with a vengeance. Sarah suspected at the time that she was pregnant, and nausea with the wild tossing of the waves added confirmation. She spent much of her time in bed in the captain's cabin. During the storm the stowaway disappeared. The first mate ordered a search, scouring the *Emma Marr* from top to bottom. When no trace of the boy could be found, in desperation the mate asked permission to search the captain's cabin. Jimmie had hidden himself under Sarah's bed, where he cowered, pressing his hands tightly over his eyes. The first mate removed him by his hair. Later, another great lurch of the ship sent the boy running back under Sarah's bed, where kind Sarah allowed him to remain until the weather calmed. Sarah smiled as she remembered Jimmie's pleas to be taken into the McDonald family. The law required that Jimmie, a minor, be returned to Ireland on the next boat.

As soon as Sarah was certain that she was to have a baby, John wrote to his mother asking her to locate a suitable house for the growing McDonald family to purchase. The first time they returned to a Canadian port, John and Sarah traveled to Sydney and inspected several residences. The third home they visited belonged to a physician who had installed steam heating, a most unusual convenience for the late 1800s. After freezing in her travels back and forth on the Atlantic, Sarah noticed the furnace first and then the charming leaded glass windows, the carved panelling, the open fireplace in each room. The McDonalds purchased this house to be used by Sarah and baby Jack whenever a voyage seemed too difficult for a child to make. John made it clear to all that this was Sarah's house to do with as she pleased. He regarded downtrodden women with distaste and adored the strong-willed girl he had married. The respect she demanded of the crew on board the *Emma Marr* sometimes amazed him, and occasionally he wondered if she might not be as exacting a captain as he.

✳ ✳ ✳

Sarah gazed at her newborn son, smiling as she imagined
John's reaction to him. Pride would shine in her husband's blue
eyes, the same loving pride with which he regarded her whenever
he introduced her to crew members or friends. How lucky she felt
to have such a mate, a man who respected her independence,
her intellect, who asked her advice and valued her opinions.

Now Sarah lay in her bed with the blue satin draperies in
her steam-heated house waiting for her sailor to come home.
Baby Jack stirred beside her. Had there ever been such a
handsome boy? Hearing the whimper, Flora McDiarmid tiptoed
into the room and took the infant from his drowsing mother.
Looking at Sarah, her black hair spread on the pillow, the hint of
a smile playing at her lips, Flora wondered if the future could
possibly be as eventful as the year since Sarah's marriage.

Chapter Seven

"A son. I have a son." Relief flooded his mind as Captain John Alexander McDonald read and reread Sarah's letter. "Strong, healthy, with a loud, lusty cry and of course thick black hair." A McDonald trademark—no surprise, that. "Now there are two of us awaiting your return." Sarah wrote.

"My darling wife and now a son," the captain thought. "If only the letter had come yesterday. Then I would have handled young McLean differently."

John had been told of a drunken excursion on shore. With a day's pass, two of his crew had spent their time at Maria's, an establishment of poor reputation. McLean had brought a bottle to the house and in an inebriated frenzy, had broken glasses and furniture. He was returned to the *Emma Marr* bound, his hands tied behind his back, to confront his angry captain. Concerned about darling Sarah, upset at being so far away from the impending birth, John felt total disgust and fury with the young man. He had repeatedly stamped on McLean's feet until the first mate's shouting finally penetrated his rage. Some bones in McLean's feet were broken. Why had he attacked a member of his own crew?

His Presbyterian background and an abhorrence of liquor were certainly responsible. But what of his abhorrence of violence? Never mind. Soon Sarah and their son would sail with him. "I am a better man with Sarah at my side. Yesterday could not have happened with her aboard my ship."

Reaching for a pen, John tried to decide whether or not to confess his disciplining of McLean in a letter home. He certainly felt more comfortable whenever Sarah could share his distress. "But this is no time to burden her with my troubles," he thought. "A new baby is enough worry, and today the doctor seemed to think the feet, though broken, would heal properly. I must never again cause physical injury to a member of my crew. I must never again cause injury to another human being.

"What kind of boy will my boy be? A fine Presbyterian—never a drinker—a student, but strong in body as well as mind. I won't mention McLean to Sarah now. I'll tell her someday, some distant day when the time seems right."

✳

Darling Sarah,

We sail for home at dawn. I will pray for strong winds and friendly waves and will greet you and our young son before October ends. I feel your love when I am alone, and nightly search the heavens knowing you do the same.

I am tired, Sarah, and need to spend some time with my dear family. Never forget your sailor. He will never forget you.

John

✳

Captain John McDonald watched his first mate go down the gangplank to disappear into the crowded streets in search of the last of the twelve-man crew. With the next tide the *Emma Marr* slipped into Atlantic waters toward home.

The harbor lights in Halifax greeted the weary mariners as they completed their long voyage from South America. The captain's eagerness to return had led the sailors to set the sails to catch every hint of favorable breeze, and they had made record time. Now as John placed his Bible in his duffle bag and knotted the string, his thoughts flew to Sydney and another John Alexander McDonald. Just a few more days and he would see his son, hold him in his arms, and embrace his darling wife.

Weariness engulfed him, and regret that McLean's punishment had marred an otherwise perfect voyage. On their return had his crew's respect been tinged with fear? He hoped not. He would look backward no longer. The future awaited him in Sydney. As soon as the crew had unloaded the cargo he would turn his paperwork over to Mr. Francis Tufts, the *Emma Marr*'s owner, and be on his way home.

Sarah, cuddling baby Jack, rested on a quilt on the grass as John approached his little family. Unaware of her husband's return or his hurried footsteps, Sarah hummed to herself, dreaming of her first sight of Captain John Alexander McDonald. She touched Jack's mass of black hair and straightened the collar of his sailor suit. "Soon your father will be home, my boy."

"Sarah." Astonished at the rush of feeling which stole her breath, Sarah could hardly grasp John's hands as they pulled her to her feet and into his arms.

"The baby!" She spoke into his uniform, crushed against his heaving chest.

John gently released his wife and reached for his firstborn son. Sarah had dressed the infant in the uniform John had sent, even though it was several sizes too large. John smiled at Jack's quizzical expression. "Young man, you inspect your father just as he examines you. Sarah, bring the blanket and I'll carry Master McDonald into the house."

✳ ✳ ✳

Long days at home before his marriage had often stifled John and driven him to long, lonely walks beside the Sydney River. Now the captain valued each day of the six weeks before his next assignment. He dreaded leaving. Jack wasn't really old enough to sail long distances and the *Emma Marr* was bound for Brazil again. How could he abandon his handsome son? How could he live without Sarah? What was the song she so often sang, "But men must work and women must weep." He almost felt like weeping when he sailed away from his wife and baby son. Just one more voyage.

Chapter Eight

Two years passed with repeated journeys from Halifax to
South America, and the *Emma Marr*'s reputation for reliability grew
with each completed voyage. Now Mr. Tufts wanted to sail to
St. John, New Brunswick, the *Emma Marr*'s point of registry, with a
load of coal. Lumber, their usual cargo, held no fear for Captain
John. Coal was another matter, for volatile coal dust often
exploded. Many ships had been lost when rough seas disturbed
the cargo. And to complicate matters, Sarah insisted on joining
him on this trip. Her fierce Scottish determination asserted
itself as she stood, hands on hips, to announce her intention.

"You have sailed two-and-a-half years without us. Jack
deserves to try his sea legs, and I deserve the company of my
husband." Unknown to John, Sarah also suspected another
pregnancy and wanted the backdrop of a star-filled night on the
Emma Marr to share her news.

John had never opposed Sarah in any of her desires. If she
wanted to sail to St. John, let her. But an uncomfortable
foreboding hovered over the captain and his crew. Winter winds
on the North Atlantic always blew cold, and dangerous tides
and currents made navigation difficult. The coal in the hold
seemed a black omen. And the worry of having the owner
aboard added to the gloom. One of the old crewmen complained
that a woman brought bad luck.

On the third night out, all hands on deck fought constant strong wind and heaving waves as the ship entered the passage between Seal and Mud Islands. Suddenly, a mysterious rumble echoed through the hold. Sarah had been lying on the bed next to her sleeping son, reading the 46th Psalm:

> *God is our refuge and strength, a very present help in trouble. Therefore will not we fear, though the earth be removed, and though the mountains be carried into the midst of the sea; Though the waters thereof roar and be troubled, though the mountains shake with the swelling thereof. . . . God is in the midst of her; she shall not be moved: God shall help her, and that right early.*

A thunderous explosion suddenly shook the cabin. Sarah reached for Jack's clothes as her now wide awake, pajama-clad son ran to discover the cause of the tremendous bang. Throwing a woolen shawl around her shoulders and still clutching her Bible, she hurried after him.

Upon entering the smoke-filled gangway, Sarah heard Captain John's voice shouting orders as she saw the first mate scoop little Jack into his arms and carry him up to the deck. The ship was sinking fast, and Sarah followed the first mate with her heart hammering. The first mate held her son as Sarah measured with her eyes the distance from the deck down the rope ladder to the lifeboat below. She had never noticed how high on the water the *Emma Marr* rode. And now the ship rocked with gale force winds. John was suddenly beside her and seeing her hesitation and fear, he squeezed her hand and hummed in her ear, "Pull for the Shore." How well she knew that tune, almost lost in the wind. Knotting her shawl under her chin, Sarah tucked the billowing skirt of her nightdress into her pantaloons and began the downward climb. The first mate followed, carrying

Jack. True to his responsibilities, Captain John remained on board until the last of the crew found a place in one of the two waiting lifeboats. Then, with a final glance at his beloved *Emma Marr*, John gave a sharp salute and joined his family.

From her corner of the lifeboat Sarah watched the pale faces of the crew as they struggled with their oars. Her thin, wet nightdress offered no warmth, and the mood of the men offered little encouragement. Still shivering, Sarah hugged Jack close and looked around. Her husband, the first officer and his nephew, Mr. Tufts, and four sailors shared her lifeboat. The rest of the crew was crowded into the other small lifeboat. The two boats stayed together at first, but mountainous, crashing waves forced them to separate. They all expected that rescue would come soon, since they found themselves in the well traveled "Track of Ships." But after hours passed with no ship in sight and the sea growing rougher by the moment, even Sarah wondered if they would be rescued. No one knew of their plight.

In the midst of the storm, Sarah remembered the words of the psalm and felt that a loving Father had prompted her to read that particular scripture to give her courage in this adversity, "though the waters thereof roar and be troubled."

Over the thundering of the waves Mr. Tufts shouted, "Someone sing something." There was no response.

"Mrs. McDonald, I hear you humming round the decks sometimes. Sing something."

"Mr. Tufts," Sarah protested through chattering teeth, "I don't know of a song unless we try 'Pull for the Shore.'"

Sarah and the ship owner sang three verses of the old Salvation Army song: "Pull for the shore sailor, pull for the shore. Heed not the rolling waves but bend to the oar. Drear was the voyage sailor, now almost o'er. Leave the poor old stranded wreck and pull for the shore."

Captain John winced at the words. Referring to his proud, lovely *Emma Marr* as a poor old stranded wreck was too much. This song, a secret signal between him and Sarah, had always been sung in a lighter vein, a private and fond communication. Sensing the captain's distress, the sailors stopped rowing.

Immediately Sarah commanded them to continue. Nightgown plastered to her skin, hair streaming in the wind, chilled to the bone and trembling, Sarah spoke with the voice of authority, and the crew obeyed. Sarah, eyes blazing and chin held high, recited the words which ran over and over in her mind: "God is in the midst of her. She shall not be moved. God will help her and that right early." The sailors were not God-fearing men, but as the captain's wife, shouting over the roar of the sea, quoted a comforting scripture, their courage returned. Soon all hands began to sing, "Pull for the Shore."

The high seas swept them into the Bay of Fundy, where the tides were the strongest in the world. Little Jack slept in Sarah's arms, unaware of the dangers threatening him, for the current carried the lifeboat away from shore and even the strongest pulling on the oars did little good. Once more, Sarah began to sing, this time alone. No one else in the boat had the heart for it. Sarah remembered the promise in the psalm. She thought of the new life within her. She couldn't falter.

Finally a light appeared—another ship! They all joined voices and together shouted into the gale. Those on watch heard them and soon strong hands lifted Sarah as she tried to climb aboard the ship, too chilled to grasp the rope ladder, too tired to see the anxious faces looking down on the little lifeboat. Later, warm, dry, and dressed in a sailor's uniform, Sarah knelt by her bed, thanking her Heavenly Father for the scriptures, for inspiration to read the 46th psalm, for faith to believe, for a courageous husband, for little Jack, and for the new baby. In the confusion of the storm, she hadn't yet told John that she was pregnant. She determined to find him immediately and whisper her certainty that she would bear a little girl, a little girl to be named after the *Emma Marr*.

Next morning, they were brought into Yarmouth, Nova Scotia, where they boarded the steamer *Alpha* that landed them safely at St. John, New Brunswick.

✳ ✳ ✳

Mr. Tufts complimented the captain on his courage in the face of disaster, but after their rescue from the crashing seas of the Bay of Fundy, John's spirits became as dismal as the leaden skies. The depression which attacked Captain John even before the little family returned to their snug home in Sydney was a reality. Even little Jack, now a sturdy, intelligent three-year-old following his father wherever he went, could not pierce the gloom which engulfed John.

Removal of the captain from active duty was required by law until a thorough investigation of the tragedy could be completed. Mr. Tufts had explained that because they were dealing with a British insurance company the length of time involved might stretch into months. He said that John should not be unduly concerned because he, as the shipowner, could testify that all had been done to safeguard life and the *Emma Marr* and her cargo. Still, John had become strangely silent, averting his gaze whenever his anxious wife caught his eye. Only the birth of little Emma Marr seemed to rouse the captain from his moodiness.

If Sarah felt discouraged she turned to her Bible, knowing that almost certainly she would open the book to a scripture offering consolation. John as the son of a minister had grown up with daily scripture reading and never sailed without his own Bible. He once briefly had held up a voyage when he discovered his scriptures missing, sending a cabin boy to a nearby bookseller to buy a Bible. This volume always sailed with the ship. It was a talisman to him. No gale could threaten his strong faith in God's word. Yet as the months stretched into a year since the shipwreck, John again plunged into the depths of despair.

Sarah wondered how she might help him. Talking about the loss of the ship obviously darkened his mood. Ignoring the shipwreck accomplished nothing. The sinking of the *Emma Marr* seemed to hang in the air between them, torturing John and filling him with self-doubt. Should he give up the sea? Would the *Emma Marr*'s owner decide to dispense with his services? Why had he not heard from the board of inquiry? Was he in disgrace? What more could he have done?

Sarah opened her Bible, aware of the pacing footsteps in the room above her as John asked himself these questions over and over. She remembered the promise of the psalm, "God will help her, and that quite early." Somehow she was comforted knowing that if help was to come quite early, it must come soon.

For the first time in months, Sarah felt a surge of new hope, a sweet assurance that all was well. Rocking Emma Marr's cradle with the toe of her shoe, Sarah hummed to herself as she planned dinner. It must be a beautiful dinner, a celebration, because she knew without a doubt that a change was about to come into their lives. Sarah thought of the thick vegetable and lamb stew her mother made on special occasions, and why not a trifle? Misty-eyed, she remembered her mother filling a glass bowl chanting, "A trifle of this and a trifle of that makes a perfect dessert." Suddenly, Sarah was recalled to the present by a businesslike knock at the door.

A uniformed messenger stood on the stoop, cap in hand, clutching a large brown envelope. Immediately the words echoed in her mind, "God will help her, and that quite early."

Seating the young man in the parlor, Sarah ran up the polished stairs, envelope in hand. "John," she called. "John, oh John." Ecstatically, she threw herself into the arms of her astonished husband.

He soon recovered sufficiently to tear open the envelope and read to himself: "Captain John McDonald. This letter is to inform you that after a thorough investigation by Lloyd's of London, this commendation was voted and duly noted for your actions in attempting to save your ship, the *Emma Marr*. As a result of your valor no lives were lost. We take pleasure in requesting you to report to your new command."

John descended the stairs, thanked the messenger, carefully closed the front door, and leaned against the frame. Sarah held her breath as she scanned her husband's face for some clue to the contents of the letter. Had her help come "quite early" or were their troubles multiplied? Suddenly grasping her hands, John whirled Sarah round and round the entry. "Pack your satchel, darling Sarah, you are about to take a sea voyage with your husband, captain of the fine ship *Parametta*."

McDonald Family: *Emma Marr, John Alexander, Jack, and Sarah*

Chapter Nine

A short time after Captain John Alexander McDonald was assigned as master of the *Parametta*, he was offered and accepted a position with a larger shipping company based in England. When John reported to the Leyland Line office in Liverpool, he was given two choices: He could remain captain on a sailing ship like the *Emma Marr*, or accept a position as an inferior officer on the *Armenian*, a steamship. During the long months of waiting for his name to be cleared, John's frustration had grown, realizing that the ships of the future would be powered by steam. How many times had he lain becalmed with the crew desperate for any breath of a breeze to fill the sails? He knew he must train until he understood the workings of a steamship, but he still felt greatly irritated at his enforced absence from the water, with precious time lost. If he had used those idle months to learn about the fast steam-powered vessels, Sarah and the children could join him almost immediately. As it was, if he became third officer, Sarah must remain in Sydney virtually on her own for a year.

Which choice should he make? He hardly hesitated, knowing that his progressive and independent wife would vote for steam without a backward glance. He returned to his boarding house filled with thoughts of their marriage. Sarah would say the loss of his ship had opened the door to his promotion. If the *Emma Marr* had not gone down it might have been years before this great opportunity presented itself. His darling Sarah believed implicitly in the divine direction of their lives, never doubting, never questioning. And so he wrote:

✳

Darling Sarah,

Our plans have changed. I am about to sail as third officer on the Armenian, *a steamship, until I can obtain my papers as a steam captain. Of course this will mean that you and the children must wait in Sydney for a while. The* Armenian *visits no Canadian ports, but be assured that you will see me at every opportunity. I know that I leave you in God's care, and pray that you and Jack and little Emma Marr will feel my love. Everything I do is for you.*

John

✳

Lexie had come to Sydney to help Sarah prepare for the move to Liverpool. Impatient to begin packing, Lexie wondered why her elder sister seemed content to take the children on picnics, long walks, and other pleasant pastimes while so much work waited to be done. When John's letter arrived announcing the change of plans, Sarah seemed serene and unsurprised.

"Sarah, it's almost as if you already suspected you weren't going to move until later," Lexie complained. "However do you look into the future? You always seem to know things."

Sarah smiled to herself. How could she explain to her sister that she felt so close to John, even when he was away, that she could almost read his thoughts. She loved him so very much. He was a fine man, full of integrity and devotion. His affection for his family gave him such a strong desire for their welfare and happiness that Sarah knew he would never hurt them, could never do anything unless he thought it was for their best interest. What luxury to possess a future full of love and joy!

Sarah asked her mother to allow Lexie to spend the year with her and the children in Sydney. Lexie, now a vivacious fifteen-year-old, would benefit from the Sydney schools as well as provide company for the McDonalds and help for Sarah. Flora agreed without hesitation, for Alexia, her youngest child, seemed to exhaust those around her. Lexie's constant enthusiasm and joy for life delighted but tired her aging mother.

Sarah, Lexie, Jack, and Emma Marr settled into a pleasant routine of family life. A daily maid named Elsie added to their comforts, and a cook, Mrs. Ferguson, kept them well fed. Mrs. Ferguson, a recent Scottish immigrant, had lost her husband to illness on board ship, so the McDonalds became her only family. Jack and Emma Marr found themselves without their father yet surrounded by four indulgent females determined to satisfy their every whim. No two children in Sydney were more loved, more pampered, or more praised, and their laughter echoed through the house.

But in the evenings with Elsie gone, Lexie studying, the children asleep, and Mrs. Ferguson happily polishing her copper pots, Sarah allowed the pain to come, the hollow loneliness which was hers when she thought of her John, so far away. She remembered watching him under the stars silhouetted on the bridge of the *Emma Marr*, the weeks in Ireland, the proud way he had stood with his ship sinking beneath his feet. She recalled his fierce tenderness, the warmth of his strong arms. And she wept her private tears. "Oh John," she called softly. "Oh John, I miss you so much. Oh John, my John."

✳ ✳ ✳

In the last watch of the evening Third Officer McDonald silently paced the deck. Moonlight bathing the Atlantic waters made night seem day. How enormous the stars were, how calm the sea. "I seem to be the only man alive, the only human in this place." Turning, he said to himself, "Was that a woman calling? No, I so long for Sarah that I am imagining her voice." He thought of his darling wife, his dearest joy. "Six more months, Sarah, just six more months. Can you hear me Sarah? Only a little longer."

Chapter Ten

The McDonald household in Sydney rocked with excitement. Not only was Captain John expected at any moment, give or take thirty days, but wedding plans now added to the gaiety. Mrs. Ferguson, Sarah's cook, had always attended each and every church function planned by the local Presbyterian congregation. In her devotion to her religion she had become acquainted with a widower, Angus McLeod, "a lonely man without another soul on God's earth to call his own," as Mrs. Ferguson explained.

One thing led to another, and now betrothed, the couple saw no reason to postpone a wedding. Sarah was delighted that her devoted servant planned a new life of her own, and a feeling of relief accompanied her good wishes. John was coming home to arrange their move to Liverpool. Sarah knew Lexie would be welcomed at home, but had worried about Mrs. Ferguson, who vowed never to leave Sydney. How could she support herself without the McDonalds?

The wedding offered a perfect solution, and the few flowers for the altar, a new dress for Mrs. Ferguson, and tea and wedding cake in the church parlor seemed little payment for her cook's loyal devotion. Jack would be ring bearer and little Emma Marr flower girl. Sarah hoped that John's arrival might precede the ceremony, but had grown accustomed to making her own plans, without depending on John or anyone else. She hummed as she wrote a list of purchases to be made before the wedding. Strange, she could not stop thinking of the lullaby her mother always sang over the cradles and as she worked about the house. "For men must work and women must weep."

After her brothers had taken over most of the farm responsibilities, Big John McDiarmid decided to join forces with his cousins who owned three fishing boats sailing off the northern banks of Newfoundland. On the farm, food was plentiful, but cash scarce, and Big John had always loved the sea. Compared to work in the fields, fishing to him seemed no labor at all. Flora was lonely now that her husband was away so often and couldn't wait for Lexie to return to the McDiarmid farm.

"For men must work and women must weep," Sarah sang again. But this woman isn't going to weep, she thought to herself. I have everything to make me happy—a devoted husband, two wonderful children, and a promising future across the sea.

One gnawing worry occasionally crept into Sarah's subconscious. Years before, her father had often implored his cousins to give up the sea life and return to the land. Almost in jest he warned them of the dangers of fishing off the northern banks, where in winter ships often sailed away to be seen no more. Sarah absently wondered what tragedy or joy the future held for her dear father. But in the rush of plans for her cook's wedding the dangers of Newfoundland's coast were soon forgotten.

Mrs. Ferguson made a blushing, tearfully happy bride, and, hilariously, Angus McLeod made a blushing, tearful bridegroom. Jack proudly held a lace pillow on which reposed a shining gold ring. Little Emma Marr clutched three yellow roses surrounded with baby's breath. Hardly more than a baby herself, the little girl stood with solemn dignity until the ceremony ended, then carefully handed the flowers to the astonished minister, before running to the safety of her mother's skirts.

The wedding cake, baked with care by the bride, tasted as good as it looked. Hot tea "warmed the cockles of their hearts." There I go again thinking of my father, Sarah scolded herself. As if Big John couldn't take care of himself, she thought, Big John who had always been a strength to his family and friends. "For men must work and women must weep," Sarah hummed as she walked with the children toward their home. She had loved the warm, snug feeling that pervaded their little house here in Sydney. Now her house had been sold and in four short weeks the McDonalds were to sail to England. What furniture should they leave in Sydney? John had told her that the shipping company would allow them to take a few of their favorite things. All my things are special to me, Sarah thought. All my things are favorite.

The front door opened as they started up the walk. John was home. But why wasn't he smiling—John who had been gone for almost a year?

"Sarah, darling, oh Sarah, I am so sorry." Sarah saw tears standing in John's blue eyes. "Sarah, it's your father. His boat left the banks with two others. There has been a terrible storm. Your father is lost, Sarah. Big John is gone."

For men must work and women must weep. For there's little to earn and many to keep while the harbor bar is moaning.

Chapter Eleven

Sarah, Jack, and Emma Marr boarded the ship *Canada* and arrived in England in only ten short days, steaming up the great Mersey River where over the years so many ships had entered the Liverpool dock. John had sent his good friend, Captain Culpepper, to meet the family, knowing that his own ship would be away.

When the captain announced he was taking them to his home to stay for a few days, the children were ecstatic. Sarah, looking out of the carriage, thought how strange it all seemed. Even the people looked different.

A high tea awaited the travelers at the Culpeppers'. Jack, accustomed to thick slices of buttered bread, carefully examined the crustless, paper-thin open-faced sandwiches, finally holding one up to the light trying to see through it. And the room was so cold . . . didn't the English know how to heat a home, Sarah wondered?

Soon the McDonalds rented a house on Berry Street, and Sarah ordered the maid to keep a fire burning in each room. Without Mrs. Ferguson, Sarah found herself doing her own cooking. The kitchen was large and welcoming but had no stove. Bravely Sarah attempted to prepare her meals in the huge open fireplace but often forgot to settle the coals so the kettle sat straight upon them. How many times did the pot tumble into the fire and ruin the dinner?

Sarah guessed it was the kitchen that convinced John to buy the fine house at 64 Oriel Road in the Liverpool suburb of Bootle. The large parlor boasted fireplaces on two walls that greeted Sarah's guests with a welcoming blaze from both sides of the room. Every day at tea time the doorbell began to jingle, and the room, warmed with firelight, soon filled with friends and acquaintances. Mrs. Ferguson had taught Sarah to make delicious doughnuts, and the combination of warm parlor, steaming doughnuts, and hot tea proved irresistible.

Their house on Oriel Road stood only three doors from the Bootle Town Hall with its wonderful reading room filled with well-chosen books and current magazines. Sarah often wished she could leave her guests and spend a quiet hour there reading. Sarah still felt uncomfortable surrounded by strangers with city ways so different from her own. Once, a tall, blond visitor with a smelly cigar attempted to explain to her that the best people in Liverpool lived on roads, not streets. "And the roads must be named after old colleges: Merton Road, Trinity Road, Oriel Road." She hoped that either he or the cigar would go out.

Every day at twelve o'clock noon a body of fifteen policemen called bobbies, all over six feet tall, wearing smart blue uniforms and carrying themselves like royalty, marched past the McDonald house, a miniature changing of the guard. Police Court, also located in the town hall, rivaled the drama of the theatricals often held there, such as a performance by a soon-to-be famous comedian from Scotland, Harry Lauder. A lanky, uncouth looking youth, he sang rowdy street songs that delighted his audience.

One day after Sarah had shown the last of her guests to the door she sank gratefully onto the sofa, hoping for a restful hour before her two children returned from school. No sooner had she closed her eyes when the doorbell announced the arrival of another visitor. Carolyn, the maid, came into the room accompanied by a tall ship's officer, a stranger, looking for a quiet place to stay while his ship was in port. John had told him that the McDonalds had plenty of room.

Regretfully, Sarah invited him to sit down and have some tea. His name was Joseph Wallis, his home was in Penzance, Cornwall. Tiring of his studies for the ministry, he had run away to sea. "And I have never regretted it," he exclaimed with feeling.

Sarah sipped her tea, wondering how to explain to this very splendid gentleman that if he sought a quiet place to stay, the McDonald home on Oriel Road definitely was not the answer. Lost in her own thoughts, she did not hear Mr. Wallis' question.

"I'm so sorry. What did you say?"

"I asked if there were any Mormons in Liverpool, Mrs. McDonald. We welcome Mormons on board our ship. That old superstition that any voyage with Mormon missionaries will be a safe voyage I believe to be true. When Mormons are passengers, I always ask them to my cabin to discuss religion. Mrs. McDonald, I think the Mormons are the only people in the world who live right."

Chapter Twelve

For young Jack McDonald, his father's long absences dragged on interminably. Previously away eight months for the Boer War, Captain John now commanded the steamship *Virginian* which did not even call at Liverpool. All the house's occupants except Jack—the servants, his mother, his sister—were females, and the announcement that Mr. Wallis, so impressive in his officer's uniform, might stay at their home pleased the boy immensely. Sarah's hesitation at welcoming a stranger into the family vanished as she watched her son talking to the new boarder.

"I've just had my feet in the oven in the kitchen. They were starved from standing at the cricket match," Jack declared. Sarah explained to the man that "starved" was a Canadian term that meant extremely cold.

"I used to go to St. John's School where the headmaster, Mr. Kaye, believed in using the cane a very great deal," Jack continued. "My father is a ship's captain and took me away from St. John's. Now I go to Christ Church on Hawthorne Road. I have a position of trust. It is I who carry the Monday pennies to the Town Hall every week."

Jack paused and examined Mr. Wallis' countenance to make sure he was suitably impressed.

"Next year if I win a scholarship, I shall be entitled to free use of the baths and all athletics."

Mr. Wallis solemnly looked into the boy's face. "Those who would arrive must pay the price, Jack."

At this point, dinner was announced and Sarah felt grateful to Mr. Wallis, so thoughtful of her lonely son that he regaled him with sea stories throughout the meal. Now she understood why her husband had said the McDonalds had plenty of room for this ship's officer. When Mr. Wallis found a friendly port on Oriel Road, Jack discovered a hero.

One evening, with the children upstairs in bed, Sarah invited the new boarder into the living room for coffee. "I want to express my thanks for your kindness to my son," she began. "It is difficult to be both father and mother to the boy. My husband comes home only twice a year."

"Please, Mrs. McDonald, it is I who must thank you for your generous hospitality. I get along with both the children splendidly. And it may be of interest that I have found my Mormons at 42 Islington in a very poor, very low quarter of Liverpool."

With irritation, Sarah recalled that Mr. Wallis had boldly stated that the Mormons were the only people who lived right. "What fault can you find with the way the McDonalds live?" she inquired.

"Here," he said, as he handed her several small pamphlets entitled "Rays of Living Light," by President Charles W. Penrose. "Read these when you have a little time. They will answer your question, and they won't hurt you."

Sarah recalled her religious training, which was such an important part of her childhood. Never a day passed without the Bible being read aloud to the entire family and no food was consumed before a prayer of thanks had been offered. And John's father, an ordained minister, had felt just as strongly about prayers and scriptures as Big John McDiarmid had.

How could this stranger question her beliefs? I'll let him talk but I won't respond, Sarah decided. If he will be kind to Jack who so needs a man's influence in his life, I'll tolerate these strange ideas.

"Mrs. McDonald, I have invited the president of the mission, Francis M. Lyman, to visit me here on Thursday. Will it disturb you if he comes and brings a few of his associates?"

"I shall be happy to welcome your friends into my home," Sarah replied, thinking that she might enjoy an hour at the Town Hall reading room while Mr. Wallis entertained his guests. "Just let the cook know how many are expected, and she'll provide refreshment."

Forty-two Islington indeed. Climbing the stairs to her room, Sarah wondered if Mr. Wallis realized what a dangerous neighborhood the Mormons had chosen. With their poor reputation, it was probably the only place they could rent. She was sure when Mr. Wallis associated with them further, he would lose interest.

Chapter Thirteen

Sarah waved Mr. Wallis down Oriel Road. With his proud
bearing and handsome uniform he drew admiring glances. Yet in
a way she was glad to see him return to the sea. Jack, not
wanting to be the only male in the house, had been devastated
at his leaving. "Even the cat is a girl," he complained. But Sarah
wondered how John might respond to a parlor full of Mormons.
Not that she could find fault with any of them, although her
mother would have called them a "mixed bag." Mr. Lyman was
the kind of person to be noticed in any group, a tall, strong,
intelligent gentleman. His helpers were Joseph Eckersley, Arthur
McDermott, Caleb Haws, and Alex Buchannan, and they had all
refused her tea. Sarah colored slightly as she recalled her
humiliation. They had refused politely, she had to admit, but
refused nevertheless.

All English people drank tea, and the McDonalds were no
different from anyone else, except as Canadians they didn't
drink as much tea or as often. Never one to hesitate expressing
her thoughts, Sarah asked Mr. Lyman his reason for turning
down a delicious hot cup of tea on a cold day.

His pleasant smile softened his words, "We believe it isn't
good for us."

Sarah thought of the people she knew who drank tea. They
all seemed content. Some of the very old fisher folk in Canada

lived on nothing but tea and toast. Except for a few missing teeth, they were very healthy specimens. She decided this belief belonged in the same category as Mr. Wallis' comment on baptism—something to be overlooked. After that disastrous afternoon, even Mr. Wallis had stopped drinking tea. He made her feel uncomfortable in her own home. Yes, she was pleased to see him leave.

Sarah remembered the missionaries' discussion on baptism by immersion. This subject seemed to fascinate Mr. Wallis, who produced his Bible and checked every reference quoted. Remembering the frozen rivers of her home in Nova Scotia, she wondered if anyone ever joined the Mormon Church in Canada. She doubted it. The missionaries' American accents and expressions certainly seemed out of place in Liverpool. However, no McDiarmid ever turned away a stranger, even a Mormon, without food.

At the thought of her mother, Sarah reached for writing paper. Was it really over a month since she had sent a letter home? With Mr. Wallis at sea, the children at school, and the maid taking the afternoon off, Sarah and the cook were alone in the house. Judging from the delicious fragrance emanating from the kitchen, the cook was busy baking the brown loaves of crusty bread which daily graced the McDonald table.

At last a moment of peace and quiet, thought Sarah. Time for a letter and a nap. Emma Marr was often troubled with earaches, and Sarah felt exhausted after the previous night spent applying hot cloths to her daughter's head.

"Dear Mother," Sarah wrote.

The doorbell rang insistently. Sarah could see two tall young men in black suits standing on the stoop.

"Is Mr. Wallis at home, please?" the boy with glasses inquired. "He invited us to call on him, and we have come a very long way."

Of course Sarah opened the door wide and ushered them into the parlor. No daughter of Flora McDiarmid ever turned away a stranger without feeding him, she thought, particularly not a stranger who said he had traveled a very long way. You'll have to wait for your letter, Mother, while I feed the strangers within my gates.

Once burned, twice shy, Sarah asked the cook to bring thick slices of hot bread and butter and plenty of milk. At least she wouldn't be embarrassed by having her tea turned down today. Examining the two young men, Sarah was reminded of her own brothers who ate the great "doorstops" of bread with the same relish as these Mormon missionaries did. As soon as the food had been placed before them, they made no further attempt to discover the whereabouts of Mr. Wallis, she noticed. The bread and milk captured their complete attention. It was Sarah herself who brought up the subject of Mormon beliefs.

"Mr. Wallis told me that I have not been baptized properly. I am a Presbyterian. He said that the Mormons are the only people who live right."

The missionaries eyed their hostess with some trepidation, still eating buttered bread and drinking milk without pause.

"My husband's father was a Presbyterian minister," Sarah continued. "My family never let a Sunday go by without church attendance."

Still no reply.

"How many days since you have eaten?" she finally inquired. Both elders raised two fingers, not missing a bite. Sarah, accustomed to helping her guests feel at ease, wondered what she might say to make these Mormons comfortable, although they certainly looked comfortable already. Her son's "Halloooo" sounded from the kitchen, announcing his return from school. Jack McDonald, a strong, dark, muscular boy with a ready smile and witty mind, loved people. When he discovered two strangers in the parlor, especially male strangers, he settled himself at their feet.

"Where are you from and how long will you be in Liverpool? Are you staying for supper? Would you like to play ball?"

Often as she recalled that significant day in her life, Sarah wondered: Would she and Emma and Jack have found themselves journeying the following Sunday to a poor section of Liverpool, breathing air fragrant with hot penny buns, and climbing to a tiny room above a bakery to hear the gospel of Jesus Christ if her son had not arrived home from school while the elders ate their "doorstops?"

Chapter Fourteen

"They have anything but a good reputation." John's voice trembled with anger as he tried to control his emotions. He felt deep humiliation at the interference of his neighbors, who had "kindly" come to call to tell him that Sarah's virtue was in question. Sarah, darling Sarah, who had promised to be his forever—how could anyone think that another man could attract her? Deep down Captain John Alexander McDonald never denied her purity, her loyalty. But a ship's captain must be proud and strong, well thought of in his community. Gossip, malicious or otherwise, could seriously damage his career.

Worse, Sarah had not apologized. Instead, she flared at him for doubting her. "I have done nothing wrong," she raged. "How could you think I could break the seventh commandment?" Eyes blazing, head high, she had accused *him* of being at fault. Sarah, in spite of the endless procession of dark-suited men who had visited their house, had told her husband she was innocent of any wrongdoing.

Frightened as his own temper overcame his logical thinking, John slammed out of the house and walked to the nearby Presbyterian church. As the son of a minister, John always had been taught to seek the guidance of the church in times of trouble. This was certainly a time of trouble, John thought bitterly. How could his wife who had been given every luxury—a house, servants, travel, love—how could she shamelessly betray and embarrass him? He would discuss the situation with the Rev. Mr. Campbell. Knowing of Sarah's intense dislike for Mr. Campbell increased John's determination to seek out this particular minister.

When the McDonalds first arrived at Oriel Road, they were pleased to discover a Presbyterian church within walking distance of their home. Eagerly, Sarah and the children had anticipated their first sermon, only to be repelled by Mr. Campbell's hateful and negative remarks. After a month's regular attendance, Sarah sought other religious ties.

A small Baptist chapel nearby offered a friendly congregation of humble people who made the McDonalds feel at home. Scandalized that his wife would attend a different denomination, John insisted that she remain a member of Mr. Campbell's flock. Sarah reached a compromise and each Sunday alternated between the Presbyterians and the Baptists. Now as John poured out his frustrations to Mr. Campbell, he wondered that the churchman seemed so delighted with their troubles.

"You must control Mrs. McDonald, Captain. Do not allow her frivolity to destroy all you have worked for throughout your life. She must be chastised—taught a lesson. I shall speak to her myself."

John shuddered as he thought of Sarah's reaction to Mr. Campbell's criticism. She disliked the man and felt that he had none of the love of Christ, the milk of human kindness she had associated with their other ministers in the past. And accepting advice had never been easy for Sarah. Even when she respected the advisor, Sarah resentfully tended to go her own way. John smiled as he thought of his darling wife whose determination never faltered. How had this conflict begun? John realized Sarah was right about one thing—he *had* sent

Mr. Wallis to her door and Mr. Wallis had brought the
missionaries. John wanted no trouble with Sarah. So seldom
was he in Liverpool that the thought of marring his leave with
unpleasantness seemed sad. He thanked Mr. Campbell and
returned home, anger cooled, love reaching out for Sarah.

Climbing the steps, he saw that someone had attached a
newspaper article to the front door of the house. John read,
"Beware of the Mormons. They are after the women of Bootle
and have already captured a ship captain's wife. Men of Bootle
WHERE ARE YOU?" The article, crudely torn from a newspaper
page, proclaimed that a group of anti-Mormons had invaded a
Mormon meeting and the resulting confusion required the
services of the police. A Mr. S. G. Thomas was quoted as saying
that the Mormon monsters must be crushed and their doctrines
thoroughly exposed. Never before had the McDonald home
been desecrated with signs or approached by anonymous
enemies. And it was Sarah's fault!

Once again John's anger overcame him. He threw open the
door shouting, "Sarah, Sarah. Come here at once!" He heard a
muffled sob and spun around ready to continue his tirade.
Huddled in a corner wondering what calamity threatened her
world sat his heartbroken daughter. Gently he lifted the little girl
and carried her upstairs to her bedroom. Settling into the
rocking chair, father and daughter silently clung to each other.
"I have already lost one Emma Marr," John thought. "I shall
never lose another."

Chapter Fifteen

Sarah stood at her open front door watching the retreating figure of the Baptist minister, Mr. Lloyd. He had arrived shoulders bowed, face full of concern, as if there had been a death in the McDonald family. A well-meaning member of the congregation had apprised him of Sarah's attendance at Mormon meetings and of the steady stream of missionaries who spent evenings in her parlor.

"I know at least two of them in the Bootle section of Liverpool, Mrs. McDonald, and they are up to no good."

When Sarah informed her visitor that indeed there were *more* than two in the Bootle district and if she had her way their flock would be increased by three McDonalds, the storm broke—such epithets from so gentle a man! And Sarah's inquiry as to the source of his information only further infuriated Mr. Lloyd. He snatched his hat from the hall tree and hurried from the house without even a "Good day."

Next it was the Presbyterian minister's turn. The Reverend Mr. Campbell came on three occasions. During the first visit he announced in most solemn tones that no one could be a Mormon and keep the seventh commandment. Sarah haughtily informed him that her mother had taught her from the cradle the importance of guarding one's virtue. No Scot pursued sex outside the marriage bed. "I consider your remark a most cruel insult, Mr. Campbell," Sarah coldly declared as she showed him to the door.

On his next call Mr. Campbell adopted a different strategy, telling Sarah how he admired her excellent qualities and proposing that she join the teaching staff of the children's Sunday School. Sarah had little use for hypocrites and pointed out the fallacy in asking one who allegedly broke a very important commandment to teach the young, impressionable members of his flock. When Mr. Campbell invited her to his wife's Tuesday afternoon tea, Sarah stiffly announced that neither she nor her family drank tea because it was contrary to Mormon belief. Observing the apoplectic expression on the minister's face and remembering her mother's stern advice that she must always be a lady, Sarah added sweetly, "Thank you very much for the invitation. I appreciate your thoughtfulness."

On his last visit, Mr. Campbell brought reinforcements, three ladies from the church's charity circle. Sarah greeted the quartet with courtesy and invited them to sit down. Each of the ladies repeated unhappy tales she had heard of the Mormons. Sarah knew from firsthand experience that the gossip was invented by fearful neighbors . But when Mr. Campbell fell on his knees, arms upraised imploringly, and called to God to forgive Sarah of her sins, Sarah thought enough is enough. Often, while listening to his sermons she had tried to analyze her negative reaction to this little man (and he is a little man thought Sarah—little and small and mean). Now as he knelt in her parlor praying for her forgiveness, asking that she might turn away from her terrible sexual sins, Sarah struggled for control.

I must not make an enemy of Mr. Campbell, she thought, biting her lower lip. I must not say what I am thinking. I must respect John's wishes and retain my place in the community.

". . . and help her go her way and sin no more," Mr. Campbell concluded.

The minister rose to his feet and gazed up at Sarah's angry face.

"Mr. Campbell, my Father in Heaven knows that I remain unspotted from the world. My parents fled Scotland with hardly more than their faith in the Almighty. They have raised six God-fearing children of whom I am one. Every day of my life since I was a little child I have not only read but I have diligently studied my Bible. Certain passages in the scripture caused me to wonder, but never have I doubted my Father in Heaven. One Sunday I climbed the back stairs of a bakery to listen to a message from God. For the first time in my life I heard the truth of his gospel spoken with authority—never mind that it came from the mouth of a redheaded youth dressed in a shabby suit; never mind that the benches were worn. In my heart the Lord has blessed me with a deep testimony that this is his true word and the only way to return to him, one Lord, one faith, one baptism. If my friends shun me, if I have ruined my good name, I cannot deny the truth. I have been brought up in the Presbyterian faith, and my family for many generations attended that church. I am grateful for my knowledge gleaned from the scriptures, for it was this knowledge that allowed me to recognize the true gospel when I heard it. Now Mr. Campbell if you must pray for someone's forgiveness, please pray for your own." Astonished at her lengthy and impassioned speech, Sarah turned and, mustering all the dignity in her possession, flounced from the room.

Captain John Alexander McDonald (left) and unknown acquaintance

Emma Marr, Sarah, Jack

Chapter Sixteen

Looking around the little yellow bedroom in her mother's house in Sydney, Sarah wondered how long she had sat rocking in front of a dying fire. John's letter, lying on the rag rug at her feet, confirmed that she was not dreaming. So few words to announce his final decision. "If you won't give up the Mormons, you don't need to come back to England."

She recalled that terrible day, the last time she had seen the Rev. Mr. Campbell. How furious John had been when the little minister had repeated Sarah's declaration. Her husband's anger had inspired her to implore him for permission to be baptized, unwisely thinking that nothing could increase his hostility.

"You are already baptized, Mrs. McDonald, and don't forget it." He never called her Mrs. McDonald. Instantly, she should have understood the depth of his feelings.

"Oh please, John, only let me be baptized," she had repeated.

John had stormed out of the house, probably to call on Mr. Campbell. It was so unfortunate that Jack had left a tithing receipt on the bureau in his bedroom on this day of all days. When John realized that family funds were being sent to the United States, his fury increased. His wife's deplorable behavior toward the minister followed by his son's misuse of his money with his own wife's approval inclined him to be even more deeply embarrassed when Captain White good-naturedly complained of Sarah's "Mormonizing" his wife, Bessie.

Bessie White, Sarah's closest friend in Liverpool, had four sons and a baby daughter. Her love for the boys was obvious, but her baby girl seemed to give her special pleasure. One day, from no apparent cause, the infant died in her crib. Inconsolable, Bessie became ill. The doctor feared for her life. Then Bessie dreamed that her little girl came to her holding a book in her hands, the book of Ether. The next morning, Bessie rose from her sickbed and, dressing hurriedly, walked to the nearest bookstall. No one there had heard of the book of Ether. All over Liverpool she sought the volume, sure that in its pages she would read a message from her little daughter. After days of unsuccessful searching, she called to tell Sarah of her discouragement. While sitting in the McDonalds' parlor, with tears streaming down her cheeks, Bessie noticed an open book on the table in front of her. Absently she turned the pages of the leather bound volume and to her amazement saw the book of Ether.

"Sarah, why didn't you tell me you had it?" Bessie accused. "I have searched all over Liverpool and written to London and no one ever heard of the book of Ether." Then she related her dream.

Sarah, still not baptized, bore her testimony of the truthfulness of the Book of Mormon. She had read it from cover to cover four times, learning more with each reading. Sarah urged Bessie to contact the elders. Before her husband returned to Liverpool, Bessie and her four sons had entered the waters of baptism.

"How lucky you are, Bessie," Sarah's voice held a tinge of envy. "Your husband has never been interested in religion and probably does not care which church you join or if you attend.

John has respect only for the Presbyterians. He will not allow me to join the church of my choice, the true church."

Captain White felt grateful that his wife had recovered both her health and her positive attitude toward life. In a way his complaint at Sarah's Mormonizing his family was only a thank-you. John Alexander McDonald considered it another terrible embarrassment caused by Sarah. How could she continue to humiliate him, her loving husband who only wanted her happiness? The Mormons were a cult of unsavory reputation.

Still, he knew that Sarah had always been stubborn and likely to follow her own mind regardless of his displeasure. Possibly if he showed less hostility to these people, her interest might flag. He determined to let the issue rest as much as he could.

Ten years passed in somewhat of a truce. As long as this new religion was not discussed, love between John and Sarah continued intense and ever new. Was it the long separations which made their time together so sweet—sweet if no one mentioned the Mormons? Sarah had promised to attend the Presbyterian Church with John whenever he was home. Yet as soon as the captain sailed away, Sarah and the children returned to the little rented room on Bidder Street, despite his strong antipathy.

John's pride in his children was apparent. Sarah sometimes disapproved of the elaborate dresses he purchased for Emma Marr, whose adoration for her father knew no bounds. Sarah suspected that silks and satins were unhealthy for her daughter and dressed her in the plain garb of their Canadian heritage whenever Captain John left Liverpool. The parrots and monkeys he brought for Jack found new homes at the zoo. One of the parrots insisted on calling, "Ship ahoy there matey," incessantly from dawn to dark. The monkeys had eaten three of Sarah's best hats. But life was good for the McDonalds. Even after fifteen years of marriage, Sarah felt that dreadful longing ache for John whenever he was away and she was alone.

However, with nightly Mormon meetings at the McDonalds', Sarah seldom found herself alone. Emma Marr, a gifted pianist, played all the now familiar Mormon hymns, and the elders, lonesome for home, sang with her. After President Lyman's recall, a new president, Heber J. Grant, arrived with his wife, Emily, and four daughters. President Grant told Sarah that as a child he had been unable to carry a tune, but he had practiced determinedly until he developed that skill. Now at the McDonalds' his voice raised loudly in hymns of praise with the other elders of Israel.

Sarah's neighbors never acknowledged these gatherings, having decided years ago that she was a fallen woman and that Emma Marr was well on her way to emulating her mother's despicable sexual behavior. President Grant preached in the McDonald home almost every Wednesday evening, and Sarah and the children considered this special meeting their spiritual feast of the week. And it seemed only natural that on occasion elders should begin to board in the McDonald home for days at a time.

Sarah never stopped begging her husband's permission to be baptized. She felt it dishonest to join the Mormons without his knowledge, and President Grant counseled her to wait for John. One day after a particularly bitter religious discussion John shouted, "Go ahead and be baptized if you will."

"Do you mean it, John? May I truly be baptized?" Sarah could scarcely believe her ears.

"Yes, and be damned." Bitterly John spit out the words. Captain John McDonald who never swore on his ship now swore at his wife.

"Then I will," Sarah replied, "but I will never be damned for it." With a swirl of skirts Sarah stomped from the room, slamming the door to emphasize her feelings. Lying in bed Sarah waited for John, dear beloved John, generous, caring, tender unless someone mentioned Mormons. The bedroom clock chimed, marking each hour. "I'll tell him I love him. I'll apologize for my anger. I'll bear my testimony," she said to herself. But as dawn tinted the morning sky, Sarah finally admitted to herself that her husband had returned to his ship without even saying good-bye.

Though exultant at John's giving his permission for her baptism, Sarah knew it was a hollow victory. She longed for her husband's support and understanding, yet proceeded without it, determined to go forward alone. Emma would later write, "Mother's conversion was instantaneous on hearing the gospel. We children had faith enough in her good judgment to accept what she believed and taught us. Later on when we were old enough to think for ourselves we wondered about it and pondered. The evidences in our minds multiplied as we read and prayed until the deep-seated conviction came to us that this was indeed the only true church on the face of the earth."

Jack and Emma never forgot the discomfort of lying to their father when he unexpectedly returned home on the very morning of their mother's baptism. Afraid of their father's wrath, they disclaimed any knowledge of their mother's whereabouts, guiltily torn between the two parents they loved.

During this period John could not see that the doctrine of the Mormons was any different from that of the Presbyterians, yet he resented his family's wish to affiliate with such a poorly regarded group. After Sarah's baptism, he became even more hostile toward the Church and spent much of his time when in port in Liverpool closeted with the Rev. Mr. Campbell. The most difficult realization for Sarah was her growing awareness that the husband who had almost worshiped her now thought that she might be deranged or certainly fallen from grace.

One evening following a visit with Mr. Campbell, John suggested that Sarah and the children should visit Grandma Flora in Sydney. Sarah felt certain that the family relationship was improving. Her husband had lately treated her with gentle consideration and certainly more affection than had been his recent habit.

As he helped his family to their cabin on board ship, John's manner seemed almost cheerful. Later, standing at the rail waving to him below, Sarah's mood darkened. She could not rid herself of a terrible feeling, a premonition that never again would she see her John. And as the ship moved with the tide, Sarah reached across the water toward her husband, knowing that with each splash of the waves he was slipping further away.

Chapter Seventeen

Sarah struggled up the walk to her mother's front door, thinking she had never before in her forty-five years of life been so tired. She wondered absently if anyone had died from exhaustion working as she now did at the Sydney Hospital. Her teaching skills benefitted her little as she scrubbed the stone floors on her hands and knees. She hardly noticed Flora McDiarmid with fire in her eyes and hands on her hips, angrily waiting to confront her.

Not wanting to upset her mother, who was both ill and elderly, Sarah had not mentioned her baptism into the Mormon faith. The McDonalds attended Halmouth Street Presbyterian Church weekly, paid their pew rent, and sang in the excellent choir. Occasionally, Emma Marr played the organ, sharing her rich musical gifts. The nearest branch of the Mormon Church, three hundred miles distant in Maine, accepted the McDonalds' tithing and fast offerings, but attending meetings there was out of the question. Sarah believed that it was better to affiliate with any Christian church than to waste the Sabbath doing nothing.

Wondering why her daughter and the children scratched out a living in Sydney instead of returning to their luxurious home in Liverpool, Flora had written to Captain John. His scathing reply documented Sarah's fall from grace, her rudeness to the Presbyterian minister, her refusal to obey her husband.

All the bitterness John felt found its way into this letter to his mother-in-law. Flora had heard many salacious stories about the Mormons and the things they did to women. She could not fathom the reason for her daughter's strange behavior. Sarah's family for generations valiantly lived according to the Presbyterian faith. The Scottish people, noted for loyal monogamous relationships, never indulged in sex outside marriage. And some felt disapproval of marital relations altogether, regarding procreation as a necessary evil. Could Sarah really be a loose woman?

As she watched her eldest daughter approach, she felt no sympathy for her obvious exhaustion. If Sarah was tired she had brought it upon herself. Flora eagerly anticipated telling the members of the Presbyterian women's society, the Christian Temperance Union, of which Sarah was a leading member, that they clutched a viper to their bosoms.

"Sarah, I command you to give up that terrible religion and return to your husband." Flora could not wait for Sarah to enter the house before giving her a Scottish blessing. "You know you should always obey your mother as long as she has breath, and I'm telling you to take the children and go back to Liverpool. You are not welcome in my house. No Mormon is a daughter of mine. If you think I can accept a traitor, when our family for generations has been loyal and true, you are wrong. What would your father say, Sarah? Shame, shame, shame, shame."

Sarah stared blankly at her mother. She was so tired she didn't seem able to take in the fact that her mother felt more for her church and tradition than for her daughter and grandchildren. I'll rest, Sarah thought. I'll just lie down for a few minutes until I am able to explain to my mother. If I tell her of the strong testimony which has been given to me, she'll understand. She'll be proud of me for standing up to John. I know that my husband will someday join the Church. He'll be lonesome and want to see the children and his darling Sarah. Our marriage has been too intense for him to be able to walk away from his family without a backward glance. I never would have continued to attend Mormon meetings against his will if I had not known without a shadow of a doubt that he would see the light and be touched by the Spirit. When Mother hears my side of the story, her bitterness will disappear. If I can just rest. I'll bear my testimony. I'll explain the apostasy and the restoration after I rest.

In the next few days Flora alternated between hurt silences and loud, lengthy recriminations. Bitterly, she had announced to the Christian Temperance ladies that Sarah had fallen from grace and joined the hated Mormons. Both blessed with strong Scottish tempers, mother and daughter allowed their emotions to govern them, and wondrous loud discussions resulted.

On the following Sunday in the Halmouth Presbyterian Church, the minister rose to his feet, pointed to Sarah and her children, and announced that no one in the congregation should associate in any way with the evil McDonalds. "Don't speak to them. Do not sell food to them. Avoid any association with these traitors who have turned away from God. If you value your families, stay away from this Magdalene."

"It's no use," Sarah told Emma and Jack. "We can't stay with your grandmother, and the little wage I bring home will not buy a roof over our heads."

"I can work at the Sydney mines," announced Jack. "Don't worry, Mother, I'd like to get a job."

"And I'll be a bookkeeper," Emma added. "You know how good I am at mathematics. If we try, our Father in Heaven will bless us even though our earthly father turned away. And Mother, if we move from Grandma's house, I can be baptized. I can be a real Mormon."

Chapter Eighteen

During her five years in Nova Scotia, Sarah felt like dressing in funeral black much of the time. Had it really been five years since she arrived in Sydney where John's letter waited at her mother's house? "You must choose between the Mormons or me," the letter had commanded. "Don't come home until you have severed all ties with that sect." She could not comprehend her mother's attitude when she had discovered their affiliation with the Mormons. Flora McDiarmid always welcomed strangers, any strangers, and loved her neighbors. Why then turn her daughter and two grandchildren from her home with nowhere to go, refusing even to say good-bye?

But the Holy Ghost whispered to Sarah and reminded her of cousin Mary O'Leary who ran a boardinghouse nearby. If Mary could tolerate all the drunken miners living under her roof, might she not welcome three sober Mormons? Long ago Mary O'Leary had given up her own religion and had not attended a Presbyterian meeting for years. But she never forgot the teachings of Christ, and she shared her all with friend or stranger, opening her boardinghouse to those who could not always pay, feeding and clothing those she found in need. If Sarah and her children were Mormons, what did it matter? Mary urged them to come to her, offering the McDonald's her front parlor for a home.

Sarah hoped that they would find in this neighborhood a few kind souls who would accept them for the God-fearing people they were. Sarah, overwhelmed with her cousin's generosity in offering the McDonalds the best room in her house, hugged Mary warmly, tears wet on her cheeks. But they had scarcely unpacked their few belongings when a loud knock sounded on their parlor door. "I'm going to use the phone." A fierce looking, bearded giant shouldered his way past Sarah and settled into a comfortable chair. His blackened fingernails and the gray cast to his skin proclaimed him to be a worker in the Sydney mines. Before their visitor had concluded his conversation, two jovial Irishmen entered the room, animatedly discussing a dog race they had just witnessed. Sarah hoped this parade of strangers might be a bad dream from which she would soon awaken. When a fourth gentleman came gently weaving into the parlor and collapsed on Sarah's bed, she thought, "Either the telephone or the McDonalds must go—best room indeed."

It now seemed incredible that after a few short weeks, Jack entered the mines, Emma enrolled in school, and Sarah became Mary's "right hand man." Sarah discovered that the imperious manner that had inspired her husband's crew to do her bidding also worked well with the rough miners. Soon the authority with which Mrs. McDonald commanded the boarders resulted in pristine language and courtly behavior, at least when in the McDonalds' presence.

Ever since receiving John's letter telling her to give up the Mormons or remain in Canada, Sarah had begun carrying on regular silent conversations with her husband. These continued until her death. So terribly lonesome was she and so accustomed to feeling his caring warmth that she told him of her fears, her weariness, her small victories. She did not speak out loud, but there were few nights after her work was done and the children

asleep that Sarah had not called out to John in her mind. When
Emma was teased at school for being the Mormon girl, it was
John to whom Sarah spoke about her sadness. When Jack
through his athletic prowess had become the most popular boy
in his class, Sarah's thoughts had turned to her husband with
whom she mentally discussed each day's events.

Unknown to Sarah, whether on the bridge of his ship or
walking through empty rooms of their home in Liverpool, John
too reached out to his beloved spouse: I went to a Mormon
meeting today Sarah. Ever since Mr. Campbell advised me to
write to you and tell you not to come back unless you gave up
the Mormons, I cannot bring myself to sit in his congregation. If
I had ever dreamed that you would not reply, never could I have
sent such a final message. Mr. Campbell claims that if you loved
me you would turn from that hated sect. He didn't understand
my strong, darling Sarah. So I climbed the shabby stairs behind
the bakery and sat on the back row of the sacrament service.
Two inexperienced young men led the singing, prayed and
spoke. I thought of our lovely church, the rolling organ, the
white robed choir. Discouraged, I left the hall before the meeting
ended, knowing that never could I enter with enthusiasm into a
religion so different from the church of my youth. But Sarah
darling, I will do anything to get you back, to have you come
home to me. Please write, for I cannot correspond with you. A
man must have his pride. I am so alone, darling Sarah. Why
don't you send some sign? Why won't you come back? John
sank to his knees beside Sarah's empty, unused bed.

Carefully, Sarah folded the letter from John, the letter that
had changed her life. Her first reaction on reading its bitter
message was to thrust it into the fire. Then when she realized
that this gray sheet of paper was her last tie to her husband,
Sarah decided to keep the letter because it was written by John.

Chapter Nineteen

Jack's becoming a miner had made all the difference. Emma's bookkeeping in a textile business after school kept food on the table. But the men who labored in the Sydney mines, tunneling far under the waves of the Atlantic, were rewarded with premium wages. Now they could move from Mary's, where Jack slept in the cloak closet tub and Sarah and Emma shared a narrow bed.

A Rabbi Gordon and his family occupied the main floor of a newly painted house in a convenient location. Sarah rented the upstairs, grateful for privacy at last. Occasionally, people inquired how she liked the haunted house. She tried not to think of the implication. Finally she asked her greengrocer, Mr. Ferguson, what he meant by "haunted house." Hesitantly, he explained that a murder had been committed in the building. The owner, not wishing to live where a crime had taken place, moved the home to its present location, painted it a different color, and hoped for newcomers in the community to rent it. So the Gordons and McDonalds innocently became involved in a terrifying situation.

As Orthodox Jews, the Gordons accepted the McDonalds, caring little whether they were Mormons or Presbyterians. Sarah, conscious of their religious tenets, lighted her neighbors' fires and took care of any small household emergencies which arose on the Jewish Sabbath. Often Sarah and Mrs. Gordon toiled side by side, enjoying each other's company as they scrubbed and polished. Sarah still worked part time at the hospital, and one night after the late shift she returned to discover Mrs. Gordon sitting in the darkness alone on the top step of the stoop. Sarah glanced at the light in the upstairs window, knowing that Jack and Emma were home.

Confused that Mrs. Gordon stayed outside in the night, hugging a ragged blanket and rocking to and fro, she asked, "Mrs. Gordon, please come inside immediately and tell me what is troubling you." Gently, Sarah pulled her neighbor to her feet. Mrs. Gordon violently shook her head no. She could not speak. Her eyes widened with terror, her mouth opened and closed, but no sound escaped her lips.

Sarah guided Mrs. Gordon inside the little house and helped her into bed. Whenever Sarah stood to go to her own quarters, the shaking and the rocking began once more. Rabbi Gordon finally came home and relieved Sarah of her vigil. After a week of bed rest, Mrs. Gordon told this story:

The sun had shone into the little parlor, and she decided to do her mending while the day was so pleasant and warm. She knew that all three McDonalds were at work, so when she heard heavy footsteps on the stairs she thought she should check to see if an intruder had entered the house. As she peered up the staircase she heard several pairs of running feet but could see no one. A bloodcurdling scream followed, then more running footsteps. Mrs. Gordon clutched the blanket she had been mending and went outside to wait for someone to come home. As soon as Rabbi Gordon realized what had happened he gathered their belongings and moved to a downtown hotel.

Uneasy and unsure whether to believe the "ghost story," Sarah decided that their limited budget allowed either for the haunted house or Mary's boardinghouse. Stay they must, and stay they did until one evening as she sat on her bed the curtains covering her clothes closet suddenly blew out into the room. Sarah knew there was no draft to move the drapes, and as she watched horrified, the curtains slid open, revealing the entire contents of the cupboard. Then and there she decided to raise the money to move to a house that was not haunted. But when nothing unusual transpired after several weeks, Sarah forgot her fears, until one evening at dinner the three McDonalds heard a racket in the next room. Together they rose, followed the sounds, and as they watched in amazement a small table rose of its own accord and moved near a window. Then a chair slowly lifted into the air and came to rest next to the table. Sarah was convinced. She rented another flat the very next day.

The McDonalds' new landlord, Mr. James McLean, lived a Christlike life and loved his fellowmen. His wife, an invalid, enjoyed Sarah's visits and plied Jack and Emma with candy from her husband's employment. The McDonalds appreciated such genuine affection. Condemned to a bedridden life, Mrs. McLean bloomed with the association of another woman and the pleasure of fine young people such as Jack and Emma Marr in her home. The McDonalds had begun to attend church with Mr. McLean. With no Mormon meetings available, the Bible classes and choir music seemed a special treat. The pastor never welcomed them, never even said "Hello," but the McDonalds were content to share the scriptures and listen to the hymns. When two elders knocked on the McLean door, the McDonalds felt ecstatic. Sarah had been baptized, but Emma Marr, although almost eighteen, had never entered the waters of baptism. (Jack, working away from Sydney at the time, would be baptized the following August.) Finally priesthood holders stood before them. June 5, 1912, found two missionaries dressed in white shivering on the banks of the Sydney River waiting for

Sarah and candidate Emma Marr, who soon arrived with their ever-loyal landlord, James McLean.

Afterwards, James McLean told Sarah wonderingly, "I've never seen a real outdoor baptism like in the Bible. When Emma disappeared under the water, that beautiful young woman in her spotless white dress, I must tell you, Mrs. McDonald, I was really moved . . . swallowed a lump in my throat, I did."

So enthusiastic was Mr. McLean about having witnessed the little ceremony that he told friends and neighbors, whoever would listen, about the baptism in the Sydney river. Soon most of the members of their Presbyterian congregation took sides in a debate, some declaring that Biblical baptism was the correct form, others finding it outdated. The store where Emma worked suddenly enjoyed a booming trade, as curious customers asked her how it felt to be baptized in a river. The manager, delighted with the surge of business, encouraged Emma Marr to answer any questions to keep the buyers happy.

While their minister had tried to ignore the McDonalds in the past, he soon became aware that his parishioners spoke of little else than the baptism, which was suddenly a heroic event. Finally several Sundays following Emma's becoming a Latter-day Saint, he delivered a scathing sermon on sexual sin, closing with the statement that the Magdalene in their midst with her evil son and sinful daughter would do well to find another place of worship.

✳ ✳ ✳

I much prefer the sea, Sarah thought as she examined the soot dusting her white starched blouse. I am homeless and jobless at age fifty and covered with dirt besides. Crossing a continent by rail, one should wear black, only black.

As the train carried the McDonalds toward Salt Lake City, Sarah gratefully remembered the way in which James McLean had sprung to her defense. He had watched her earning a living, caring for her children, reading her scriptures, showing kindness to his invalid wife. Mr. McLean had started a petition to remove the minister. Sponsoring Sarah in the community, he proclaimed her innocence, her purity. But Sarah knew the time had come to leave Nova Scotia. They would move to Zion. She didn't know how, she didn't know when, but the certainty daily grew within her that she must gather with the Saints. Then a letter with a Utah postmark arrived. Miraculously, the elder who had baptized Sarah in Liverpool offered the fare to bring the McDonalds to Salt Lake. They would be welcome in his home until work and living quarters could be found. Elder John C. Duncan's letter began, "I don't really understand why you have been in my thoughts, but I felt I must write and send you the enclosed money." Sarah knew that once again her Father in Heaven had shown her the way, and she offered a prayer of thanks.

Chapter Twenty

Even as his family traveled across the American continent, Captain John Alexander McDonald walked a lonely road of his own. After writing the cruel letter to his wife, he experienced a heady sense of power. The Reverend Mr. Campbell reinforced the hate and resentment which filled his being each waking moment as he recalled his wife's refusal to listen to reason, her Scottish stubbornness, her rebellion. But when John realized that Sarah had no intention of returning to Liverpool under the conditions he demanded, the gallant captain seemed to remember few negative family experiences. The memories crowding his mind were of warmth and love, the excitement of reunion, his adoring children.

He had ordered the maid to clean Jack and Emma Marr's rooms, but to put nothing away. As he entered Jack's bedroom, he noted that even the tithing receipt—the cause of the bitter altercation—lay on his dresser, and Emma's piano music waited on the chest at the foot of her bed on the brightly embroidered coverlet he had brought her from Cuba. "Oh Emma, play for me, play for me," he had said so often. Many times when he returned weary from a voyage, his daughter instinctively rendered the soft music that soothed his soul. She knew that her father loved Beethoven, especially the "Moonlight Sonata." She always lowered the lights. She could play as well in the dark as in broad daylight. If she heard a musical selection once, it was hers. Oh Emma, why did you leave? "She left because I sent her away," he grimly answered.

John wandered into the room which he had shared with his wife. No longer did he sleep there, preferring the impersonal feeling of the guest bedroom. "We had a perfect marriage, darling Sarah, until the Mormons came along." John fingered the silver brushes he had brought home from Belgium. Never would he forget the look on Sarah's face when she opened the package and realized they were for her. She had called his attention to some brushes, sturdy tortoiseshell like her mother's, as they stood before a Liverpool shop window, arms linked against the bitter cold. She listed the reasons she wanted them. But John knew that his Sarah deserved unusual and beautiful objects, not just serviceable things. When he had told her that he had no intention of buying the brushes, she said little but he sensed her disappointment. Then he returned from his next trip with an ornate silver set, a filigreed "S" scrolled on the back of each brush. Sarah had picked up the largest of the four and playfully hurled it at her husband as he lay on the bed.

Brush in hand he had run from the room, Sarah in hot pursuit. They had such fun together. Where was Sarah now? Where was his only son and his sweet Emma Marr?

There were times when depression seemed to smother him, when ugly dreams woke him from a tortured sleep and he determined to write to his wife, to beg her to return. But then he thought of his crew. Would they still respect him if they suspected he had grovelled to a woman, begging her forgiveness? And what of the Rev. Mr. Campbell? John didn't really like the man with his arrogant ways, his hateful prejudices. Still, John was afraid of Mr. Campbell, aware of the damage he had done to Sarah's reputation, knowing he could do the same to him.

No, it was up to Sarah to apologize, to mend the rift. She knew how he loved her, cared more for her than anything or anyone else in the world. And how had she treated him? What had she offered to her loving husband in return for his devotion? Even now the old anger crept over him. What an unreasonable woman he had married. If she thought he would apologize, she had misjudged his character.

※ ※ ※

Leaving Omaha, Sarah listened to the train whistle. The melancholy sound seemed just right as the engine followed the silver line of tracks across this black endless plain. Was she the only wakeful person in the car? No one stirred. Never will I think of John when others are with me. Never will anyone see my tears. I still feel that overwhelming love, that closeness, that physical bond. How can I care so deeply for a man who has turned his back on me and the children? Why do I bear this tie? It is as if one of the lines of his ship has knotted around my heart. Oh John, write to me, reach for me, remember me. Dear John, I promised to be yours forever, before I understood what it meant. This train is carrying me to a holy temple, John, a holy temple where I'll make our bonds eternal. John, John, John. Sarah covered her face with her hands and wept bitterly.

"Next stop, Salt Lake City." Sarah watched as Emma and Jack peered through the train window searching the blackness for any sign of Zion. White and yellow lights winked back at them, then blurred on the rain-splashed glass. The train was definitely slowing, the wheels no longer emitting the seesaw clackety clack that had lulled them across the country.

Sarah smiled as Emma asked her brother how many D words he could think of describing Salt Lake City. A, B, and C had been disposed of on the vast plains of the Midwest. Emma loved word games and with her prodigious vocabulary could best anyone but her mother. "Dirty, dank, depressing, dismal, disreputable," Jack intoned, "dumb, damp, disorderly . . ."

"Stop!" Sarah implored. She needed no such words to describe the city they were to call home.

"Sorry, Mother, we were just trying to pass the time, and I must have my little joke." Jack's sideways glance took in the grim set of his mother's lips, the lifted chin. "Anyway, it's time to gather all our worldly goods, all three suitcases full of them." Ever gallant, Jack's joviality revived Sarah's flagging enthusiasm. She wiped the steam from the glass with one of her enormous white handkerchiefs. The station appeared larger than she had expected. But best of all, near the back of the crowd awaiting the train's arrival stood a very tall man holding a black British umbrella under his arm. He looked familiar to her. Tears sprang to Sarah's eyes as she recognized Elder John C. Duncan who hadn't really known why Sarah was in his thoughts or why he should send her train fare to Zion.

As a smiling Elder Duncan bundled the McDonalds and their suitcases into an ancient Ford sedan, Sarah remembered their move to Liverpool and a smiling Captain Culpepper loading them into his opulent carriage. Mercifully, the rain prevented further comparison between Liverpool and Salt Lake. And then Sarah noticed surprisingly wide streets and well-manicured lawns. Everything seemed to be so clean. Zion at last, and it was not a disappointment. It was impossible to be with Elder Duncan in a small enclosed space without a hymn, and the strains of a vigorous rendition of "Oh Ye Mountains High" repeated ever louder and over and over brought the weary travelers home. "In thy mountain retreat, God will strengthen thy feet; on the necks of thy foes thou shalt tread; And their silver and gold, as the prophets have told, shall be wrought to adorn thy fair head."[2]

The Duncans had prepared one room for Jack and another for Sarah and Emma. Compared to Cousin Mary's boarding house or even the McLeans's, the privacy and cleanliness seemed luxuriant. Three wayfarers sank to their knees in humble thanks for a safe journey and Christlike friends. "For I was an hungered, and ye gave me meat: I was thirsty, and ye gave me drink: I was a stranger, and ye took me in," Sarah repeated to herself as she drifted into exhausted sleep.

✳ ✳ ✳

"Sister McDonald, here's a letter just come." Sister Duncan's warm good morning smile left no question of Sarah's welcome. "It's from England. I wonder how they knew you were here?"

Could John finally be writing to her after all this time?" Sarah's hands trembled as she took the envelope addressed in small ladylike strokes. Curiosity overcame disappointment as she carefully slit open the envelope with a knife from the breakfast table. Caroline MacNamara—Carrie who had joined the Church with Sarah, college-educated Carrie in an age when women were offered little schooling, bright-eyed Carrie snatched from the convent by the gospel net—Carrie was on her way to Salt Lake City!

Sarah helped Sister Duncan wash the breakfast dishes, then returned to the room she shared with Emma. What should she do? She had no money. Her fierce independence prevented her from accepting charity on a permanent basis. She must find a job; she must find three jobs. "For men must work and women must weep. For there's little to earn and many to keep while the harbor bar is moaning," hummed Sarah. Emma and I can work as well as any

[2] *Deseret Sunday School Song Book*, 7th edition, published in Salt Lake City, April 1904, p. 200.

man and weep as well as any woman. Sarah reached for her hat, pinned it at a jaunty angle, and went downstairs to meet the world.

The gentleman in the office of the Salt Lake Board of Education couldn't have been more gracious or less encouraging. "We can't really accept teaching credentials from Canada, Mrs. McDonald. I am sure you are well qualified but the Board has its rules, you know. If you were to go to an American college, we could hire you upon the completion of your certificate."

"Three jobs," Sarah worried as she walked along the downtown street. "Four jobs, really, if Carrie is coming." Carrie's wealthy Catholic parents had disowned her as soon as she had entered the waters of baptism. Only her impressive teaching training had enabled her to support herself in Liverpool.

The imposing white facade of the Hotel Utah momentarily distracted Sarah from her financial concerns. She admired the well-dressed patrons and, while listening to their happy conversations, briefly longed for her blissful Liverpool life. Three women in maids uniforms slipped out a side doorway. "Even the maids look smart," thought Sarah, noting their starched aprons and saucy white caps. "Even the maids—even me, even Carrie. We can make beds and empty trash into dustbins. And Emma will always find an opening for a bookkeeper. Jack can do anything and everything."

Sarah entered the lobby and searched for the personnel office.

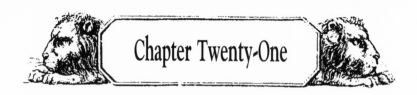

Chapter Twenty-One

Sarah's rocking chair creaked softly as she sat in the darkened living room of the little house on Green Street. She often made a fire in the tiny hearth, turned off the lights, and watched the dancing flames reflected on the walls. From the worn photograph in her hand, Captain John Alexander McDonald smiled through the shadows.

"John, your darling Sarah is so terribly tired. Every fiber of my body aches and complains with the fifteen-hour workdays it endures. And so much has happened. Wouldn't you know that Jack was the first in line to join the army for the Great War? And Emma, with your mathematical mind, John, made head bookkeeper at the Salt Lake Knitting Works. There is something now called Prohibition outlawing drinking alcohol in the United States. Emma's boss hides his liquor bottles in the underwear boxes. But John, something worse than liquor has come into our daughter's life. She has met a young man, the son of Danish immigrants who speak with an accent and cling to their old country ways. He is going to college and working as a carpenter but really has no future. Jack and I have both warned her that life with Mark Petersen would be filled with poverty and sorrow.

"There has been enough poverty and sorrow in the years since we parted. You remember Carrie MacNamara in Liverpool? Carrie came to Salt Lake City and together we became charladies at a fine new hotel in town. Your darling Sarah has scrubbed floors until her hands and knees cracked and bled. She has worked harder than any of the servants on Oriel Road. Scrubbing floors is a good time to pray; one is kneeling already. I have pled with my Heavenly Father endless hours, trying to understand why we must be separated. And my Heavenly Father has answered my pleading, John. In the downtown district of this city stands a fine granite building with spires and even a golden angel on top. You would admire the architecture. Some day you and I will be married there, married for time and all eternity. I still feel your love, John, and your Scottish stubbornness. This life is but a moment in God's plan. If we must be separated now so that we can be together forever, I can wait. Imagining an eternity with you leaves me breathless.

"Tonight I finished our story—the story of our love and the gospel that has for now separated us. My diary holds the record of the wonderful, tumultuous years that have brought us here. Someday our children and grandchildren will read it and understand. I am now content and can lay my pen aside."

Footsteps on the front porch announced Emma's return from her date with Mark. Emma knew the rules. She was to keep that young man outside. He had made a fine missionary, contacting many of her acquaintances in Nova Scotia. But even though he stayed three years he had not baptized one soul. Better to throw this fish back into the sea and try for a larger one. "John, I realize that I shouldn't discourage Emma from seeing a young man just because he is the child of immigrants. Emma is the child of an immigrant, but the McDonalds and the McDiarmids have always been educated people. It is difficult for me to talk to the Petersens. Emma works hard and with Jack's help has provided us with food and shelter. She deserves more than a future with black cotton stockings and rags.

Unfortunately, Emma is Scottish through and through. She will do just as she pleases." Sarah slipped John's picture into her apron pocket as Emma floated into the room waltzing to an unheard tune. "I don't need to ask you if you had a good time," her mother chided.

"We're going to be married, Mother. Will you let Mark come into the house after we are man and wife? You needn't worry about the arrangements. His family thinks I'm wonderful, and they've planned a wedding supper at their home after the temple ceremony. My boss has offered his cabin at Mount Air for a honeymoon. All I really need is a dress. Oh, Mother, I am so indescribably happy."

✳ ✳ ✳

Sarah and Jack had repeatedly discussed Emma's determination to marry Mark Petersen. It seemed that their objections made her even more unwavering, and on August 30, 1923, amid torrential showers, the wedding took place.

Now with the couple on their honeymoon Sarah sat fingering the delicate lace folds of Emma's wedding gown. "Most inappropriate," Sarah thought. "If you are going to choose a man without a future you'd do better to buy working clothes. Those who dance must pay the piper. How could my only daughter disregard my advice?" Sarah imagined long, miserable years ahead, Emma poring over company books until her back was bent and eyesight blurred. If she insisted on marrying against her mother's wishes, her mother would provide at least one dress to wear to work. Sarah carried the wedding gown into the kitchen and carefully dropped it into a kettle of black dye.

Chapter Twenty-Two

Emma's daughter Marian stirred in Sarah's arms as she rocked and pondered. How could I have objected to a marriage that has produced such a perfect child? Emma is happier than ever before; ambitious Mark is working at every job he can find. And Emma says that he writes well. Every day when Mark finishes at the railroad he goes straight to the *Deseret News* office and asks for work. He says they'll have to hire him to get rid of him. Sarah smiled at the baby, smiled thinking of her son-in-law, smiled at herself.

Sarah had never seen Emma so angry as when she had discovered her black wedding dress. Emma's temper had been legendary even among the rough seamen on her father's ship. And the sailors gleefully taught the curly-haired darling blue words to use in expressing her anger. Only fear of the captain had stopped this practice. Fortunately Emma was speechless at her mother's behavior. Yet six months had passed before Sarah's daughter willingly shared thoughts and affection with Sarah again. Now Mark and Emma had gone dancing while Sarah rocked her first grandchild and held John's picture.

"John, dear John, you finally broke the silence when you wrote and asked Emma to come to you in Boston at the home for retired seamen. She wanted to come, John, but she had just given birth to Marian. All the bitterness she had felt is finally gone. She realizes that you objected to the Mormons' poor reputation—that you only wanted the best for us. So Jack made the long trip, and how thrilled he was to see you again, even if it meant witnessing your death. You told him of the lonely love you still cherished for your family."

A knock at the door startled Sarah. Who could be calling at such a late hour? Most of the Green Street residents tucked themselves in by nine-thirty. The clock showed after eleven. "Sarah, it's John Duncan. I regret the hour but I must speak to you."

As Elder Duncan entered the parlor, Sarah thought he looked ill. And the ever-present smile was gone from his kind face. "Sarah, I'm in trouble. President Hinckley wants to make me a bishop. I can't be bishop without you. I know it's a large ward and a hard ward, but it's a loving ward. What do you think, Sarah? Will you help me?"

Sarah's sense of humor never deserted her. "Elder Duncan I will help you in any way I can, but surely you are not inviting me to be your counselor."

Reddening as he realized his request had been unclear, John C. Duncan replied to his star convert, "Oh, but I *am* asking you to be my counselor, Sarah. I am asking you to be the Relief Society president, the most important counselor in the ward."

So it was that on December 2, 1928, sixty-five-year-old Sarah McDiarmid McDonald became Relief Society president in the First Ward of the Liberty Stake just in time to greet the arrival of the Great Depression. Sarah's teaching talents, rejected by the local schools, already blessed both the Sunday School and MIA. All the priesthood members met by quorum for Sunday School, and as the high priests' instructor, Sarah McDonald, was particularly able. It was over a year before the stake realized that the high priests' teacher in the First Ward happened to be female. A woman teaching Priesthood! And high priests at that! But the two men assigned to investigate listened in awe as she parried questions, revealing her extensive knowledge of the scriptures. "She's a walking concordance," Brother Davis reported. "There is not a man in the ward that knows the gospel like Sarah McDonald. There may not be a man in the Church, either." Sarah was left in place.

Her first month as president began with a flurry of Christmas boxes and dinners. Drives for clothing and bedding for the poor were a challenge in a ward filled with poor people. "But we can share the little we have," thought Sarah. "The sisters need the gospel more than ever with so many of the men out of work."

The bishop instructed Sarah to present some sort of social at least every other month. Sister Hinckley offered her home for a Silver Tea, where the astronomical sum of $31.80 was donated. Cake sales in the two grocery stores within the ward's boundaries brought in another $20.00, and a birthday party added $51.49 to the general fund. Sarah gave each sister a penny, asking her to increase her talent to a dollar then return it to the Relief Society. Cash had vanished with the appearance of the Depression, and Sarah felt proud to be able to send $3.00 to each of thirteen missionaries from the ward at the end of the year. She challenged the sisters to "look around and find someone who really needs special attention. Make them happy all the way through—not a smile on the outside to cover up a tear or even a broken heart on the inside. Make yourselves happy by making others who are less fortunate happy."

She spoke often on the need to study more in order gain the Spirit, to be cheerful, and at every meeting she had the members rise and repeat, "We stand for a full attendance of our members at all meetings, offering no excuse for absence that we could not conscientiously give the Master." She arranged for the

Relief Society Magazine in every household. She prayed for those she served and saw in need: "Dear Father in Heaven, help me to know what to do about the sadness that fills the homes in this place. Many men have no work, and some have slipped into old habits of liquor. Dear Father, I remember how I felt when I needed to break a 30-year-old habit of tea-drinking. The craving for that cup of tea occupied all my thoughts. I felt weak and nauseous. Finally I decided that I must be dying. I went to bed for three days waiting for the end to come. The only thing that came was an exhilarating knowledge that I was free. No habit could rule my body or my mind. Now these brothers are trying to avoid their shame. They cannot provide for their families so they drink to forget their bills, forget their empty pockets, forget the time on their hands. Please Father, let me know how best to help them."

When ward conference was held in November of 1930 with the attendance of stake president Bryant S. Hinckley, Sarah was able to report that during the year the Relief Society had made 7 quilts, 43 baskets for the needy, and 15 Christmas cheer boxes that were sent to the aged and homebound. Four dollars had been sent to each of the 12 ward missionaries; another $16 had been added to the ward missionary fund. They had delivered 3 floral sprays to funerals, bought dainties for the sick, and given a one-act play entitled "Deacon Dubbs."

The year 1931 deepened the needs of the people Sarah served. President J. Reuben Clark issued a warning: "The poorest kept places in town will be those that are inhabited by persons who have nothing to do. Insist the recipient of your kindness do something around his own house so he will not get something for nothing—that philosophy is the most destructive influence you can bring into the lives of others. Tithe payers deserve first attention, but do not let anyone starve, tithing or not. Often a non-tithe payer has a faithful wife and family. We must have charity. We must have the patience of Job, the charity of Paul. 'Inasmuch as you do it unto the least of these my brethren, ye do it unto me.' Accumulate food and shelter sufficient for all. Help the Saints become self-sustaining. The unemployed should beautify ward grounds, varnish doors, do stonework, lay concrete, plant flowers and shrubs. Mere giving of material relief is not service."

Sarah accepted her marching orders from President Clark's talk. With the same zeal she had used on the lifeboat in the Bay of Fundy, Sarah encouraged, even ordered, the unemployed to work. Homes were repaired, cleaned, and painted; yards brightened with flowers. The ward house and grounds became a showplace. Most importantly, the unemployed held their heads high. Sarah's army was on the march to glory.

Beware if you wore a new item of clothing to a church gathering. You could expect Sarah to pounce on you with a flowery compliment on your appearance. "What a lovely new *coat*. How it becomes you. And where is your old wrap? I'm sure you'll want to share it with someone less fortunate." Who would dare say no? Sarah accumulated stacks of wearables using this method. She invited the recipients to her very warm fireside (she always kept her apartment blistering hot, remembering chilblains from Canada and England) to feast on her famous lamb and barley stew and try on clothing. When Emma asked how she could spend so many evenings with the needy, some of very dubious reputation, Sarah's chin went up as she replied, "I am overfond of children and degenerates."

If a child's red wagon was insufficient to hold the food, clothing, and fuel she daily delivered to the members of her ward, she found someone with a truck, someone with money for gasoline, and someone to lift and carry. No one—not any person young or old—felt hunger or cold during Sarah's regime, if she could help it. More importantly, pride returned to the poor—not the sin of pride condemned in the Bible, but pride in home and church, combined with a genuine self-esteem that transformed despair to hope.

If the Relief Society members were unable to pay the annual dues of fifty cents, let them come regardless. Let them participate in planting the silver and Norway maples at the Hogle Zoological Gardens (Sarah had browbeaten the two trees from an unsuspecting nurseryman, explaining that it was his duty to honor George Washington). Let them work to serve 400 chicken dinners to the hungry of the area. Let them entertain the old folks and prepare cheer boxes to give to the housebound.

Years before, when Brigham Young had called a Central Grain Committee led by Emmeline B. Wells, Eliza R. Snow, and Bathsheba W. Smith, Sarah McDonald was still a young girl attending school in Fourchu. These three Relief Society sisters had accepted their mission to save grain instead of buying bonnets or other finery. They raised wheat, gleaned wheat, stored wheat, and bought wheat with the proceeds from the sale of quilts and homemade foods. At the time of the First World War, the United States badly needed all the wheat they could find. As loyal citizens, the LDS Central Grain Committee and all the local grain committees agreed to sell their wheat to the government to aid the war effort. Proceeds from the sale were deposited in a central bank and the interest on each ward's share paid to them annually. Now, all these years later, this wheat interest money floated Sarah on the sea of survival. She mentally congratulated Brother Brigham on his inspiration and foresight whenever a wheat check arrived.

In each Relief Society meeting Sarah stood and bore testimony to the truth of the gospel and urged the members to study and pray. Her need for fun asserted itself in the socials, dances (15 cents admission), cake parties, plays, and songfests. Her favorite event was the Japanese Geisha Tea party at the home of the stake president. Sarah's efforts reached far beyond the First Ward's boundaries as, faithfully, each Christmas the Relief Society continued to send a small amount of money to each of the ward's missionaries. In January 1934 Sarah proudly read letters of thanks and appreciation from Elders Gordon B. Hinckley, Grant A. Richmond, and Wm. M. Harvey.

Her statistics were more than impressive. She would always remember the look on President Hinckley's face when she reported 4,698 visits to families in the previous year. Sarah's emphasis on reading of the scriptures with nonmembers had resulted in many conversions of members as well as nonmembers. And this same Relief Society president had talked a local physician into giving the entire ward physicals at three dollars each, 367 completed.

Sarah felt that the women of the ward were engaged in an uphill battle, so each Relief Society day she urged them to hold a weekly family meeting to educate themselves, their mates and their children, and never to miss Relief Society. Her twin goals of education and knowledge of the scriptures became the First Ward's battle cry. And throughout the ward's boundaries, "Sister Mac" reigned supreme. When President Bryant S. Hinckley, returning from his East Millcreek farm, noticed a boy from the stake walking along the road, he offered him a ride. The usual questions came forth: what is your name? who are your parents? where do you live? "What ward do you belong to?" President Hinckley inquired.

"The First Ward, sir," the boy replied.

"And who is your bishop?"

"I'm not sure, President Hinckley, but I think it's Sister McDonald."

✻ ✻ ✻

Six years later, whenever she visited the Church cannery,
Sarah felt overwhelmed with gratitude to belong to a church
which provided for its own. The new Welfare Square with its
soon-to-be-filled grain elevator stood sentinel against a repeat
of the hunger experienced in the last decade. As she walked
down an aisle between tall stacks of newly filled cans, Sarah
recalled the Great Depression and imagined how many meals
this new storehouse could provide. A workman had left his
sawhorse directly in her path, and while admiring the shiny
silos, Sarah did not see the danger. She tripped, fell, and broke
her hip. Two friendly strangers noted an aging matron sprawled
at their feet, ignored her protests, stood her up, and walked her
across the building to the office.

Never before had Sarah felt such pain—shooting, fiery
agony. "Stop, please stop!"

"Never mind, little lady, we'll have you sitting down in no
time."

Sarah never had been called a little lady before, but she
was in too much physical distress to object. "I want a doctor,
please, I must go to the hospital." White-faced and trembling,
Sarah convinced the office manager that she needed help. With
the two strangers still supporting her she was walked to a
nearby car, placed in the front seat, and driven to LDS Hospital.
Never would she forget that walk. Never would she forget that
ride. After surgically setting her fracture, the doctors gave little
hope for her recovery.

"John, dear John, is the time finally here? Am I to see you
at last? I still carry your photograph, John. The nurse took it
from my purse and I have put it under my pillow. I am so tired,
John, and the pain is more than I can bear."

Chapter Twenty-Three

On her high, narrow hospital bed Sarah drifted in and out of consciousness. She saw herself teaching in Black Brook. The boy in the front seat rose and stood next to her. He laid his hands on her head and promised that soon she would be well. He commanded her, with the authority of the priesthood, to be healed. She looked more carefully and saw that it was Mark, Emma's Mark. How had he arrived at Black Brook and where were all the Morrisons?

"John, can you hear me, John? I'll come as soon as I can. In just a little while we'll be together, but for now I must finish . . ." Sarah could not remember what it was that she must finish. "For now I'll just sleep."

With rest and improvement came a restoration of Sarah's fighting spirit as she mounted a recovery campaign. Never before had the nurses seen a patient so determined to walk. Any staff member passing her bed was commandeered for constant trips up and down the hospital corridor. With the courage of a true McDiarmid, Sarah fought the pain and discomfort, determined to conquer her injury. When she triumphantly returned to her tiny apartment the only change observed by watchful neighbors was that Sister McDonald now walked with a cane. Her eyes twinkled in amusement as she passed younger, slower members of the congregation on her way to church.

Six weeks in traction had afforded her unlimited study time. Beware the teacher who misquoted a scripture in her hearing. Fortunately she taught in all organizations. While she stood before a class no one worried about the accuracy or the liveliness of the material. Physically she seemed to tire more easily after the accident, but after all, her youthful mind was trapped in a seventy-seven-year-old body.

She still walked endlessly, and in her walking managed to check on the ward members who most needed help. She shared her prescription for all ills with everyone she knew: be cheerful, enjoy life, study and live the gospel.

Sarah felt her most glaring failure in her later years was with Carolyn MacNamara, her educated friend and fellow convert from Liverpool. Carrie had discovered that if she didn't work, the Church and state still supplied her needs. She saved her welfare checks and scavenged food and clothing from the trash barrels stacked behind downtown businesses. Sarah could not fathom why anyone would squander a fine mind and years of schooling and live the way Carrie did. However, early each morning, Carrie, dressed in rusty black (Sarah hated to think of where her garb had originated), trudged from her Eighth South apartment to downtown Salt Lake City. If her checks had arrived, she visited six local financial institutions where she and her deposits were well known. Still haunted by the bitterness of her family when she joined the Mormons, Carrie feared that in some way they would discover her whereabouts and take away the money she frugally hoarded. So every account was under a different assumed name—six banks, six names. Her business transacted, Carrie's next stop was the public library where she read all the available newspapers and occasionally treated herself to a few hours with her favorite author, Dickens. Then on to the trash barrels where this bent, ancient lady spread wide her two shopping bags and began to inspect the day's offerings. With her hands gloved in black lace, she delicately lifted each item for examination then dropped the approved merchandise into her bags. When she was finished for the day, she wended her way home with her plunder.

Carrie's lifestyle bothered Sarah less than her rare attendance at church. Why give up everything for the gospel, then turn one's back on it? Occasionally due to her poor living conditions and questionable diet, Carrie became ill and seemed to be dying. At these times Sarah sat with her friend recalling their splendid times in Liverpool. Who could forget President Heber J. Grant and his moving sermons, or the enthusiasm of the elders?

Carrie recovered repeatedly. She resumed her downtown forays as soon as she could drag her crepe-soled feet one in front of the other. Yet in some indefinable way Carrie always displayed the air of a lady, exuded culture in her conversation, showed interest with her snapping, black, intelligent eyes.

Carrie outlived Sarah, and even in death held tight to her six bank books. No one knew the names on the accounts, so ultimately the state of Utah claimed her hoard. She had denied herself uselessly. However, a grand funeral with flowers, music, and eulogy sent her on her way. With Sarah gone, she had listed Mark E. Petersen as next of kin when she entered the county hospital for the last time. And Elder Petersen buried her with style.

✳ ✳ ✳

In spite of Sarah's determination, walking became increasingly painful for her. When questioned, the doctor explained to Sarah that at her advanced age no one really thought she would recover when she broke her hip. Therefore, her hip repair had not been "quite what it should be." So on April 14, 1940, after twelve years of service, it became necessary to release Sarah as president of the First Ward Relief Society. At seventy-seven she was "turned out to pasture" with only two teaching jobs—Mutual and Sunday School. Her Relief Society attendance remained perfect, reminding her associates that they "should offer no excuse for absence that they could not conscientiously give the Master."

Sarah didn't resign herself to her rocking chair. She continued to aid and counsel those in need and to keep a close eye on the members of her family. She regularly corresponded with Lexie, her youngest sister still in Nova Scotia; with her older brother Matthew; and with his son Donald. Donald had settled in Hawaii where he became band leader at the prestigious Royal Hawaiian Hotel.

In 1943 Donald must have written to Sarah explaining that his son Donald McDiarmid, Jr., would be passing through Salt Lake on a troop train bound for Buckley Field near Denver, Colorado. For when the train stopped at 8:00 a.m. one spring morning, there stood Sarah, determined to meet this nephew. No soldiers were allowed to leave the train, they explained, though it would be at the depot until late afternoon. Sarah refused to admit defeat, confronted those in charge, and soon a very bewildered Don McDiarmid was hurried into a waiting car and into the arms of relatives he didn't even know he had. He spent the day visiting and eating, until finally it was time to return to the depot. A very well-fed soldier bid a fond farewell to his Aunt Sarah and rejoined his wondering comrades.

One of the delights of Sarah's later life was her close association with President Heber J. Grant. Neighbors were no longer surprised when the long, black limousine stopped in front of Sarah's tiny, red brick duplex and the chauffeur helped her into the car. President Grant could spare only an hour, but somehow the hour usually became two. When Emma asked what they found to talk about, Sarah smiled mysteriously and gave a vague answer.

Mark suspected that his brilliant mother-in-law had become a counselor to the prophet in the same way she had been counselor to Bishop Duncan. There were women in the Church who felt deprived because the priesthood was held only by men. "They weren't acquainted with Sarah McDonald," stated Mark. "She wields more power than many high priests. Her influence has redirected lives and policies. If the needed changes could not be accomplished without the priesthood, she found a priesthood holder to do her bidding. Sarah McDonald has magnified her calling as well as anyone I know." Even after twenty years of marriage to Emma, Mark still called his mother-in-law "Sister McDonald." He never quite got by her imperious manner to address her by her given name.

Sarah, the "bishop of the First Ward," continued her ministrations, visiting the sick and the troubled, guiding the youth toward goals of education and excellence, giving rousing lessons and an occasional sermon in church, all the while loving her seven grandchildren and endearing herself to them.

A serious bout with pneumonia convinced Emma that her mother should come to live with the Petersens. The illness left Sarah too weak to object, and she settled into the front bedroom in the house on Diestel Road where she could watch the world go by from her rocking chair.

Sarah McDonald

On the second Sunday of October, 1948, a new face appeared in Gordon Owen's Sunday School class in the Petersen's ward. This was not unusual, for Brother Owen, a well-known KSL Radio personality, attracted many visitors to the Bonneville Ward. With his dark good looks, smooth delivery, and meticulous preparation, his classes overflowed with intellectuals from the entire Salt Lake Valley. Sarah looked about her with interest. This class was as large as the entire First Ward! Almost everyone held a triple combination, an excellent sign. And they really listened to the teacher. There might still be life after the First Ward, thought Sarah expectantly.

Mentally she compared the vast assembly with the few Liverpool members meeting over the bakery redolent with the Spirit and fragrant bread. Brother Owen quoted the second chapter of Daniel as he interpreted Nebuchadnezzar's dream. He had forgotten the name of Arioch, the man whom the king ordained to destroy the wise men of Babylon.

Sarah's hand went up respectfully and was ignored. The waving hand became urgent, seeking attention. "Brother Owen." At age 85, tall and frail, black hair streaked with gray, Sarah McDonald rose to her feet and corrected her teacher's interpretation of the scripture before the open-mouthed group. "Oh, and the man's name was Arioch," she added with a smile.

After the closing prayer, Sarah made her way to the front of the chapel to discuss the passage with Brother Owen. A lesser man might have resented this lady clad in Scottish tweed standing before him, not only for stealing the spotlight but for adding humor to the proceedings. It was impossible for Sarah to speak before a group without eliciting at least one chuckle. She enjoyed life and enjoyed learning and she shared her pleasure with those around her. Now her mischievous blue gaze took in Gordon Owen with curiosity.

"I can see, Sister McDonald, that it may be well to examine in advance each Sunday's lesson with you. On which days do you receive?"

Mutual affection and respect grew between Brother Owen and Sister McDonald. Every Sunday School lesson discussed drew them closer together. She soon began to listen to his broadcasts, making suggestions for changes, of course. He altered his homeward route from the station so he could pass her window. And she refused to retire, regardless of the lateness of the hour, until she had seen his car and the blinking headlights that told her goodnight.

Years later, another member of the Bonneville Ward Gospel Doctrine class remembered Sister McDonald's contributions. Senator Jake Garn would recall his surprise that this old lady would correct Gordon Owen (who was regarded as a great scriptorian) and that anyone in her eighties might possess such an instant recall of wording, verse, and meaning. "I was astounded at her mental capacity, particularly at that advanced age, and her in-depth knowledge of the scriptures. If anyone read from the scriptures in that class, he had better be sure not to change even a word, or Sister McDonald's hand would go up. I can still see her raising her hand."

Senator Garn also remembered a meeting in which she

spoke at the invitation of the bishopric. He was sitting as a
priest at the sacrament table. "I recall her describing her
shipwreck, telling the sailors to 'Pull for the Shore,' of her
having the audience in the palm of her hand, of a great deal of
laughter in spite of its being a very spiritual experience."

Sarah McDonald became mentor to Gordon Owen, who
had not needed a mentor. She became watchdog for the gospel
in all her meetings, Relief Society, Sunday School, MIA. The level
of excellence in the organizations in Bonneville Ward rose to
new heights. No one dared present a lesson carelessly
prepared, knowing that Sister McDonald would be listening.
Sometimes it was difficult to tell she was not teaching, so great
were her contributions.

Her relationship with her son-in-law, now a member of the
Quorum of the Twelve and manager of the *Deseret News*, never
changed. She still told him exactly what she thought of his
newspaper, his speeches, and his lack of pride in dress. When he
cut the lawn wearing "disreputable clothes" (Mark thought the
baggy jeans and ragged sweater comfortable and the battered
hat the perfect touch for a man forced to endure white shirt and
tie six days a week), Sarah refused to introduce her well-known
son-in-law to her many visitors. When asked who the man in the
backyard was, Sarah always replied haughtily, "The gardener."

Sarah attracted the youth. They could speak to her in a way
that few of them shared with their parents. Rarely was the sofa in
her room unoccupied. Sarah helped young people solve their
problems. She raised their spirits and cheered them to success.
She listened, encouraged, and always made them laugh. She often
walked them to the corner and usually stopped to converse with
the two elderly maiden ladies living nearby. Sarah regarded them
as her missionary assignment, and with a companion or alone, she
strolled the distance, her cane helping her along. She never left

the house without an elaborate hat and gloves, a twinkle in her blue eyes, and a jaunty step. That the "elderly ladies" she visited were at least twenty years younger than she was unimportant.

This backwoods girl from Nova Scotia had firmly established her place in two of the great wards of the Church. Now she was tired. As she rocked by her window waiting for Gordon to signal an end to her day, she examined the photograph in her hand and wondered about her husband. Had he heard the gospel? Had he accepted its teachings? Her greatest disappointment was that she had been unable to be sealed to him in a holy temple. Mark and Emma traveled to the Glace Bay cemetery where he was supposed to be buried so his genealogy would be accurate, but the little graveyard was filled with John Alexander McDonalds. His work still had not been completed.[3]

A painful hacking cough finally kept Sarah from attending her meetings. She felt so very tired. The doctor thought her pneumonia had recurred and wanted to hospitalize her. She could not struggle to the window even to see Gordon say goodnight. Reaching under her pillow she felt the picture of John safely with her to the last. Why were so many people standing around her bed? "The Lord is my shepherd, I shall not want." Big John McDiarmid was rolling his r's as he recited his favorite psalm. And Big John McDonald stood nearby, arms outstretched, calling to his darling Sarah.

"She's gone."

Sarah died quietly at home. Her funeral, conducted by Elder Joseph L. Wirthlin, now of the Council of the Twelve, attracted large crowds of people who enjoyed the speakers but would have preferred a rousing sermon by Sister McDonald. The headstone in the Salt Lake City Cemetery says it all: Sarah McDonald, 1863–1957, ninety-four years young.

[3] The couple was sealed in the Salt Lake Temple on March 29, 1976.

Epilogue

Two women arrived as the taillights of the sleek, silver hearse disappeared in the gloom.

"We'll have her room spotless in no time at all. There's so little left after 94 years."

The soft blue sheets pulled easily from the bed and dropped to the polished wood floor. A small, yellowed photograph fell silently among their folds.

"Look, it's a picture of some man in a uniform. She must have kept it under her pillow."

"Handsome, wasn't he, like an actor. Look at those eyes and that old fashioned beard."

"I wonder who he was. Imagine Sarah McDonald having a romance, keeping a man's photo under her pillow."

"The picture's all cracked and torn. I bet she held it every night."

✳